DISCARD

HARD-BOILED EGGS
AND OTHER PSYCHIATRIC TALES

_____

The Rebirth of the Psychotherapy
of Severe Mental Illness

by

ALBERT M. HONIG

_____

north street publishers

Printed in the United States of America.

For further information address Albert M. Honig, Honig Associates, 616 North Street, Doylestown, Pa. 18901; phone: 1-215-348-2134; e-mail: albhon@earthlink.net; web site: http://www.dramhonig.net. Books may be purchased directly by check or money order for $15.95 through phone call,
e-mail, or from the website.

Cover designed by Duane Cosner.

Honig, Albert M.

HARD BOILED EGGS AND OTHER PSYCHIATRIC TALES: The Rebirth of the Psychotherapy of Severe Mental Illness.

north street publishers

ISBN 0-9713876-0-5

Dedicated to my best friend and live-in companion

Sylvia

This book would never have been published without the editorial help of Johanna Wilson, the assistance of Sylvia Honig, and the general support of the members of the Bucks County Writers Workshop.

Contents

Redemption And/Or Covenant
A review of Hard Boiled Eggs and Other Psychiatric Tales
by Albert M. Honig
Reviewed by Harold J. Fine

One has many, as well as enduring and fleeting reactions while reading Honig's case histories, autobiography of sort, and creativities in the psychotherapy of the very disturbed, borderline, and psychotic who couldn't or wouldn't reenter a state of grace and continue a so called sensible life internally or in the community.

So we must begin this review with the Jewish tradition to do healing as a form of salvation or giving a religious allegiance to social justice, of a soul to be restored and "cured" back to a seamless submission to an ambivalent Godhead. This is called "tikkun olam" the restoration and healing of a world. Such a passion drove Frieda Fromm-Reichmann.

Honig comes from this tradition buried as it may have been in his secular family residing in a small industrial town, provincial, and in sight of the imperial city seen a river away. Honig, the first grandchild, doted upon by an extended family where his childhood as *primus inter pares* was a benchmark of his enfolding life despite the affliction of the depression and hard times, and a daily near combat of worries and fears of falling back to even a more marginal life.

He persevered with Hebrew studies, good schooling, eagle scouts and the diversion of athletics and sports. On to the navy, medical school and a burgeoning curiosity about mental disorders probably due to a cousin's schizophrenia. A general practice in New Jersey, and seeking an analysis in

New York with Theodore Reik, then aging and ill with Honig reciprocating attending to Reik as a medical doctor. An unusual relationship for those days which may be a source for his broadening the borders and boundaries with his own patients.

These biographical notes do not yet suffice without a most significant variable. Out of the dissonance of the midwest grew many political and educational movements tied in with the anti Eastern dominance of American life. They grew with evangelical fervor. One type was the proliferation of medical schools such as chiropractic, naturopath, osteopath and though rooted in Germany, homeopathy, where the Germans of this mid-continent founded such training grounds.

Honig's uncle attended osteopathic school in Missouri thus resulting in a half century of nephews, cousins, grandchildren following his path. Honig looked upon his uncle as a model. He turned down entrance to an Ivy League medical school to attend an osteopathic school. Up to 20 or so years ago there was a degree of marginality to these professionals.

It was with this background that Honig entered a residency in psychiatry and an introduction to long term psychosis. After working with John Rosen, he went into private practice. In 1961 a clinic was opened as an attempt to build a therapeutic community model with family members living in cottages. Here, patients became residents. At first it was an attempt as a medication free environment but the community concept of the 60's rapidly brought back the re-industrialization of psychiatry. Honig's book. "Hard Boiled Eggs—" presents four cases: that of Ann, an anorexic, Cheryl and Joan, long term psychotic, classified with the garden salads of the DSM. And Max, a psychiatrist, long loopy, regressed, catatonic, and paranoid, containing an emergency stopping of all action to avoid running amok.

There are long an exhausting relationships, wearing down both patient and therapist. Small but significant progress and growth emerge, enough to leave this secular convent to engage the world in work and creating families. Except Max who flees when the clinic is in trouble fostered by dissident staff members who feel jealous and angry about this unusual treatment. Max goes up in flames as a kind of another Vietnam era martyr. There is very little theorizing, which is good as it would weaken excellent story telling.

Honig sees a psychoanalytic base. While so, it is a reach or an indebtedness to Ferenczi, and gestalt element a la Fritz Perls, and psychodrama in the fashion of J.L.Moreno. It is difficult to tease out object relation elements but that is of little significance in the story that is told sometimes painfully as Honig reacts with empathy and projective identifications, and counter transferences at times over wrought.

This messianic effect is a price brought on by the stresses of this intensive lonely work, driving him to prayers in a Catholic church, where redemption is offered. But the need is a covenant with these inscrutable protectors and punishers of the insane delusions and hallucinations. The results are a variety of illnesses: heart, tonsillitis (oral ?), and prostatitis (anal?) inflicted on the soma and psyche of the therapist.

There are a wealth of ironies. Honig is now semi retired. The clinic he co-founded has changed its name. It is now a behavioral institution making money with patients in for short stays, possibly more appropriate for the juvenile justice system than a mental health facility.

The place is replete with physicians, social workers and nurses — like many such places. There are no clinical psychologists. The dominance of the biological heredity and brain discontinuity as primary cause of human misery is preeminent. So we shall soon try to calibrate the serotonin energy and force the neurotransmitters to behave.

It is the ravages of a finance capitalist takeover, managed care, insurance restrictions, and the return via genetics of the so called medical model.

Huxley's soma of a brave new world and now Robert Cohen's new novel "Inspired Sleep" illustrates the pharmacological blurring of life and devalues it. Huxley and now Cohen use parody and satire that illustrate, and predict what happens to a Prozac, Paxil, and Zoloft universe. Even Honig trumpets the illness model obscuring the developmental deficit and stresses that are now called sick.

The wife of one of the recent presidential candidates made her mission mental illness and parity of treatment. That is okay, but what treatment? Honig is caught up too, in the semantics of illness and cure an elusive entity when faced with character structure. There is profound gain and growth via this intense therapy. This clinic born of the community health clinic of the Camelot hardly exists anymore except for administrators with fat salaries and CEO titles. Where are the Menningers, Shepard Pratts, the small intensive treatment centers on the West Coast, the Payne Whitneys? Austin Riggs is struggling, but still running, and the legacy of Frieda Fromm-Reichmann ghosts of what remains of Chestnut Lodge.

Foucault's essays on *The Birth of the Clinic* should accompany this volume to realize the contexts of Honig's writing.

We have come a bit away from this book. It is a good read, and in another time a popular and enlightening book; but it may not be fashionable to conglomerates called publishing houses.

Harold Fine is a retired psychologist/psychoanalyst, He is Professor Emeritus at the University. of Tennessee and a Distinguished Senior Psychoanalyst (ABPP)

Author's Preface

I've been a practicing psychiatrist for over forty years and, in that time, I've treated all sorts of mental disorders, from anxiety disorders to depression, to the most severe, the schizophrenias. One thing I've learned is that no one, regardless of economic status, educational achievements, or familial background, is immune from the suffering caused by mental illness.

It is hoped that this book will rectify that omission. By way of personal accounts, it will give Many people have come into my Bucks County office, and each one has a story to tell a story that, but for the grace of God, could be yours.

The statistics are sobering. Today more children seem to be affected by mental illness earlier in life. The murder and suicide rates among children and adolescents are horrifying. However large the numbers and costs may be, they cannot begin to account in human terms for the enormous emotional stress and pain borne by those with severe mental illness and by their families.

Far too many find appropriate treatment inaccessible because they lack insurance coverage, or because the coverage they have for mental disorders is inequitable and inadequate.

But statistics often mean little to the average person. And figures don't touch the heart of the matter. It is hoped the reader some idea of the immense suffering and pain caused by mental illness, and illustrate a way that, in the long run, may alleviate this suffering and be more cost effective than the methods currently in practice.

Introduction

"In the great decisions of life, "Theodor Reik, famed psychologist and my first psychoanalyst, once told me, "one must go by how one feels." I remembered that advice many times over, once I'd begun my practice, moving from family medicine to state hospital to the clinic that I founded.

My work in mental illness started in the back wards of the state hospitals, far from the early days of Freudian-fashionable psychoanalysis. The state hospitals were notorious as dumping grounds mandated to take everyone—the poor, the aged, and the needy, as well as the mentally ill. Before the current saga of the homeless ever began, the state hospitals housed the most chronic of the mentally ill, many of whom were taken from the streets.

In order to become intimate with the difficult problems of treatment, I would often steal time from my paperwork to examine patients' emotions and responses. I noticed the stubbornness with which people, long psychotic, defended their beliefs. These chronic sufferers had slipped into another place, another world, and they protected that universe as though their life depended on it. Suicide was one of their options; most, however, simply accepted their nightmare existence (which they didn't recognize as mental illness) as commonplace, a hopeless road upon which they walked.

The more time I spent with these patients, both in residency and in early practice, the more I envisioned an alternative treatment. I saw the need for a psychiatric "incubator"—a sanctuary for patients from the street, from institutions, even from prison—as well as a need, in some cases, for an experimental laboratory to break through the barriers of insanity and provide the nutrients for emotional and physical healing.

I visualized patients living in this incubator as part of a family, with married couples providing daily emotional nurturing and structural follow-up to the physician's therapeutic work.

Reduced to simple terms, a surrogate family, plus a patient, equals a hospital. If it worked, it would restore dignity to the patient, provide relief to his or her natural family, and introduce a different way to understand the mentally ill. Frustration and lack of understanding have often caused even the most dedicated doctor to lose interest in a severely disturbed patient. This new system would provide gratification to the aides and nurses who live closest to the illness. And there would be time, the most precious commodity needed by the patient for understanding and growth. The goal? A total personality reorganization, a therapeutic make-over, and not just patchwork remission until the next breakdown.

That early vision eventually materialized as The Clinic and foundation in Bucks County. This book recounts the stories of four unique people who stayed at The Clinic and became part of that vision. Three were able to return to society reborn, and with personal visions of their own.

It is with regret that I have disguised the identities of people and places in these stories. In another place and time, these people might be considered heroes for what they have suffered and accomplished. However, I hope these narratives will help the general population to understand better the cause and effect of mental illness. Increased understanding of mental illness can help erase some of the opprobrium that still surrounds it.

Chapter I
Hard-Boiled Eggs and Anorexia Nervosa

1. Fear of the Flesh

Ann refused to eat.

In fact, she considered her self-imposed famine an accomplishment. Though bent on starvation, she was preoccupied with food. Thus she saw her practice as ascetic self-discipline, a search for purity of the highest form.

She liked to exercise and would run and bicycle. Yoga was also part of her daily routine; she would set aside time in the morning and the evening to meditate, believing this practice would help her maintain control over mind and body. Lose control, she believed, and she would suffer catastrophic results. She would drive herself to perform calisthenics—stretching, sit-ups, pushups, headstands—often to the point of sheer exhaustion. Afterwards, she would happily suffer through hunger pangs because they gave her a sense of achievement. When the hunger pains vanished, her pride produced further ecstasy.

Anorexia nervosa. It is hardly a recent phenomenon. Nor is it a new condition fostered by late twentieth-century stress. In July 1684 an eighteen-year-old Englishwoman who developed amenorrhea, apparently from a "multitude of cares and passions of her mind," sought help from a Dr. Richard Morton. In "the last degree of marasmus," she had lost her appetite and her digestion had deteriorated, resulting in weight loss and fainting spells.

Dr. Morton noted in his journal that he was shocked by her appearance. "I do not remember," he wrote, "that I did ever in all my practice see one that was conversant with the living so much wasted with the greatest degree of consumption (like a skeleton, only clad with skin). Yet there

4

was no fever but, on the contrary, a coldness of the whole body; no cough, or difficulty with breathing, nor appearance of any other distemper of the lungs or of any other entrails. Only her appetite was diminished and her digestion uneasy with fainting fits which did frequently return upon her."

Morton treated this young woman with salts and tinctures. However, she would not cooperate and only lost more weight. About three months after coming to see him, the woman died during a fainting spell.

Morton, in his textbook, concluded that this disease "does almost always proceed from sadness and anxious cares." Thus he described the first case of anorexia nervosa in the medical literature. More important, he concluded that this disease should be seen as an emotional or psychiatric illness. This took place about 160 years before the birth of Freud.

Almost 200 years later, W.W. Gull neologized "anorexia nervosa" to describe young girls who refused to eat "due to a morbid mental state, weight loss, and amenorrhea."

No doubt Ann was one of those youngsters described by Hilde Bruch as being engaged in a desperate fight against feeling enslaved and exploited.

Anorexia, Bruch says, is a puzzling disease full of contradictions and paradoxes; these youngsters, who are defiant and stubborn and who impress one at first contact as strong and vigorous, willingly undergo the ordeal of starvation even to the point of extinction. But their sense of autonomy eventually gives way to an even greater enemy—death.

Anorectics panic at the thought of gaining weight. "In order to avoid that most dreaded fate of gaining weight," Bruch says, "they brainwash themselves into experiencing hunger as something pleasant and desirable."

When Ann's illness first began, she would stand for hours before the mirror making faces, thinking her face ugly, her legs fat. In the bathtub, she pushed out her stomach and invited her mother to see her "big, fat stomach."

It seems to me there is something exhibitionistic about anorexia, though few girls will admit that. During therapy, many confess they have not felt sure of anyone's love, and this cruel dieting is a way of drawing attention to themselves. Bruch has written, "Young anorectics say, 'If I eat and get fat, my mother won't love me anymore. Not eating keeps her involved with me.'"

I have always thought there is an almost medieval disdain for and fear of the flesh among anorectics; like religious ascetics, they experience a longing of the individual soul to meet with his or her God and seek a rapture that comes from transcending the human condition. Mundane human interpretations are often treated with contempt, and physicians are seen as trivializing the ritual of the anorectic's behavior and bringing it down to a formula ("You're anorectic in order to keep control of your parents"). They will often accuse the physician of not understanding the nobility of their martyrdom.

Man has always tried to understand the connection between mind and body, spirit and flesh, abstinence and sensuality. Perhaps anorexia nervosa should be viewed in this broad context.

This battle between abstinence and sensuality may have been best exemplified, in the early 1500s, by Ignatius Loyola, who founded the Jesuits. Loyola developed a system of spiritual exercises that stressed the torturing of the body to acquire perfection and sainthood, love of God over love of man. Ritualized over a four-week period, the exercises began with purging and ended in illumination and experiencing the spiritual joys of God's love. Ignatius secretly had an undergarment made for himself, consisting of strips of leather filled with 150 brass nails which had been filed into sharp points to be driven into the flesh.

Most observers today feel that anorexia nervosa has a psychological origin, but some authors point out that tumors of the hypothalamus or of the cerebellum can cause similar conditions. Although there are daily advances in the chemistry and neuroradiology of the brain, we are not yet able to signal where the separation of mind and brain occurs, nor can we tell which part of the illness to attribute to nature (genes and chemistry) and which part to nurturing (environment).

In addition to the severe disturbance in body image, the misinterpretation of internal and external stimuli, and the inaccuracy in the way hunger is experienced, anorectic patients almost universally exhibit a paralyzing underlying sense of ineffectiveness—a conviction of helplessness and an inability to change anything about their lives. It is against this background of helplessness in facing life's problems that the frantic preoccupation to control the body and its demands must be understood.

I first heard about Ann one morning after Christmas. I was in my office at The Clinic, conferring with an inpatient, when the receptionist buzzed me.

"There's a man here who wants to talk with you about his daughter," she said. She explained that he had been walking around the grounds and now sought a few minutes of my time.

The man's name was James Trumbull Sr. He was of medium build, well-groomed, with fine features, and was dressed neatly in blue jeans and a maroon turtleneck. He spoke haltingly, in the Anglicized American accent of Manhattan's Upper East Side, about his daughter and her condition.

"She's sixteen," he explained, "and is in our community hospital in New Jersey. She spent Christmas there in bed."

He went on to say that she had been a patient on a ward in a prominent large medical facility where the anorectics cared for the cancer-ridden children. "The anorectics are all teenagers or older and they must work with these sick babies, feeding them, cleaning them. I guess it teaches the anorectics that there are people sicker than they are." Before that, he said, she had spent eight months in another hospital, diagnosed with anorexia nervosa. He had seen most of the patients get well, but his daughter's condition actually worsened.

He went on to say that Ann was only four foot, eleven inches. "She should weigh ninety pounds, not sixty the way she does," he said, obviously distraught. Both he and his wife, Cynthia, wanted their daughter home, but at home she would eat nothing. In the hospital, she at least took some nourishment. This disease has a ten to fifteen percent mortality rate, and both parents were afraid Ann would die. They had tried everything, and they saw my clinic as their last hope.

I was pessimistic about the prognosis, but I gave in to Ann's pleading father, who didn't know where else to go, and I agreed to admit Ann to The Clinic.

I had never before worked with clinically diagnosed anorexia nervosa with bulimia. But I had worked with many psychotics and catatonics who wouldn't or couldn't eat in response to the commands of inner voices. Obeying these voices, they would drop to between sixty and ninety pounds, depending on height, taking just enough nourishment for sustenance. After continuing on a self-starvation regime for a period of six to eight months, they would begin to eat and drink again. Somehow they survived, knowing by instinct where their starvation tolerance level ended.

There were occasions when a catatonic would give us a fright. These patients would curl into a fetal position with all their orifices closed—eyes, mouth, rectum. It seemed as though they believed themselves back inside the womb, and all they needed to do was lie there, connected to the imaginary umbilical cord of an imaginary mother.

These catatonics were often helped by active efforts—which they usually ignored at first—aimed at rebirth: holding, hugging, kissing, rocking, and the offering of nurturing bottles. As in the process of normal fetal maturation and birth, they would miraculously emerge some ten months later.

Ann soon arrived, with her parents and an enormous suitcase, and I was shocked when I first saw her. She resembled a scarecrow. A heavy blue sweater covered a frame of skin and bone. Brittle hair topped a woodened face bestudded with sunken eyes, thin cheeks, and parched lips. Flat buttocks were stowed away inside oversized green wool ski pants. Swollen ankles pitted over the edges of her new white Nikes. She might have been a survivor of Auschwitz.

Ann's mother, Cynthia Trumbull, looked haggard and worried. Born and bred in Australia, she was a primary school teacher who had studied art and had written and illustrated several books for children. When she married she had continued teaching all through her first pregnancy. That first baby, a male, died at birth. Ann was born a year later.

At first Ann was a quiet baby, fond of her bottle.

Parental uneasiness began when Ann, who had been placed on the potty at eleven months (probably too early), began to rebel, evacuating in her diapers.

The birth of Baby James some nine months later aggravated this problem, but it dissolved some months later after bribery with candy. James, weak from birth, was difficult. A poor eater, he didn't gain, but even lost weight. But his mother was proud that, despite the doctors' gloomy outlook, she had increased his vigor and robustness through a regimen of vitamins and food supplements.

While James showed improvement, Ann stopped eating. Mother's homespun treatment of her daughter began immediately. This included daily doses of Vitamins C, E, A, B12, B6, and B2. Brewer's yeast, mixed with water into a paste, was served to her daughter two or three tablespoons at a time. With renewed confidence in nutrition and faith in its ability to cure all ills, Cynthia Trumbull had became a devotee of Adele Davis.

Cynthia was little impressed by The Clinic on that day of her daughter's arrival. "Is there an internist who specializes in children and adolescents on staff here?" she asked rather critically. "This place doesn't look like a hospital, and it's got to be filthy with germs! We must have a medical specialist on Ann's case."

"I'll call one of the internists at General Hospital and have him follow her case closely. He has had a great deal of experience with adolescents, and the hospital is only a stone's throw over the hill."

Seemingly mollified, the parents marched to the newest family unit to settle in their daughter. Cynthia led Ann to the bedroom to put away her clothes, make up the bed, and add a mother's touch in what other ways she could. They went to their car and returned with two heavy cartons of granola, chewable vitamin C, multiple-grain bread, and bottles of vitamins and food supplements. All these treasures were stored beneath Ann's bed. Six gallons of Breyer's natural ice cream were put into the freezer.

"I have all these wonderful foods and vitamins," Cynthia said sadly, "but all Ann will eat is ice cream. And her awful thumb sucking! There must be something you can do about these awful habits."

Conversation ceased at that point. Mr. Trumbull picked up a newspaper while waiting for his wife and daughter to complete what they were doing, but Cynthia and Ann were not able to unyoke. Finally he took his wife by the arm. "Come on, you've got to stop. We have to talk to the doctor in his office."

Once there, both parents sat hunched over, hugging their chairs. Ann's possible death permeated the room like a leaden cloud, and I could make no promises of cure. "I'll do my best," I said, "and we'll all work very hard. What else can I say?"

Their next words were startling. In the midst of expressing concern for their daughter, they abruptly shifted emphasis and asked for a psychoanalyst for each of them in New York City, one who might be available immediately.

I noticed an avariciousness, an insatiable inner hunger that demanded on-the-spot fulfillment. Ann's parents were needy for emotional sustenance, while Ann took in almost nothing, not even enough nourishment to sustain her. I had seen this neediness before in parents, but never so blatantly expressed. Could Ann have feared their avariciousness as an assault on herself?

The next day Ann submitted to a medical examination. Her blood pressure was 86/50, pulse 98 and bilaterally weak, heart sounds showed no murmurs, stroke volume weak. Her eyes were sunken, her pupils reacted sluggishly to light and distance. Her hair broke apart between the doctor's fingers. Her fingernails and toenails showed a lack of calcium. Her complexion was pale, her legs thin with pitting edema. Her throat and tongue were parched, skin turgor loose from dehydration.

The internist wasted no time in calling me on the phone. "Honig, what the hell are you doing?" he bellowed. "Don't you know people like this can die from heart failure if you begin to refeed them? This girl needs to be in a large hospital where she can have medical and psychiatric services combined. And she definitely needs drug treatment."

"She just came from a large hospital, doctor," I responded. "And she received all the latest medications for this condition." It seemed that my support system itself needed support.

2. Feed or Famine

Ann ate nothing during her first four days at The Clinic, and she drank only enough water to prevent fever. She did not speak until the second day, when she asked to talk with me.

"I want to leave," she whined. "There are stains on the rug. This is a fecally dirty house. My mother's house is much cleaner. I want to go home." Her voice was shrill, enfeebled. There were no tears; her body couldn't spare them.

From the beginning, I felt enormous pity and tenderness for this pathetic young person. She reminded me of a wounded baby gazelle of the African plains who could no longer defend itself and might be abandoned by its mother and the herd, easy prey for the hyenas and the jackals. Frightened in these unfamiliar surroundings, Ann sat in the middle of the room, not knowing what would come next, and with little strength to seek a corner or a couch as a hiding place.

How should I react? To reach out with compassion before she was ready to receive it would be like asking for sputum in the eye. As I looked at her face, and then around the room, I could feel the terror, unspoken but pervasive, spreading like a thick black fog. And I thought: Sometimes it is better to grab the wild bull by the horns and wrestle it to the ground!

"You've got nothing on you but skin and bone—not one piece of meat!" I shouted. "Who would want you? There's nothing on you that's good to eat. Why don't you go over and pick up the vacuum cleaner and make this place comfortable. You've no place else to go."

The apparent harshness of my voice froze her fear, and she instantly became more compliant. That day she vacuumed the house three times; the following day, she vacuumed again. But her actions held intense hostility and stubbornness. It became obvious that she wanted to control her own life—to eat what she wanted, when she wanted, and how much she wanted. She was nearing dangerous levels of dehydration but I, too, remained unmovable, and I steadfastly refused to make her starvation the focus of my thrust.

How ludicrous it all appeared! This young woman of the upper classes, angelic-looking, unassuming, and intelligent, was starving of her own volition in the midst of plenty, crying for deliverance while refusing every attempt to save her. She mocked the most instinctive expression of human concern for others, the sharing of bread, the giving of the apple. Her ordeal reached far beyond self-flagellation and the denial of the body.

Ann feared a fate more terrifying than starvation, perhaps an end more dreadful than physical death. Why were the parental gifts of life and nurturance—expressions of love—seen as sadism and mind control? To Ann's way of thinking, acceptance of love would make her a mindless robot. In a macabre reversal of the natural order of love, to deny herself the means of life was to preserve her person. The process called to mind the use the Nazis made of systematic starvation, meant to break the will and make it easier to lead their victims to the gas chamber. But who were this girl's persecutors? Yes, she was in agony, but others, including myself, also were feeling pain. Was the punishment she intended to inflict on her parents also being directed to those who lived and worked with her?

In the therapeutic home, transferences (emotions transferred from significant others in the past) soon emerge, directed toward physician and surrogate parents. Suspicion leads to accusations, which lead to displays of intense hatred and violence or withdrawal. Regression to early stages of life creates a vulnerable need for nurturing. A different sickness emerges, one that is the outcome of early infantile traumas, unsatisfying family relationships, and poor attachment formation.

I did not want Ann to die. So we flooded her with simple kindness. But compassion and Christian love were useless so long as she viewed all nurturance, physical or emotional, as a denial of her identity and as death. I began to think of myself as a (mental) surgeon with a cancer to cut out. It promised to be a dangerous operation, and painful as well, but if it was successful, the result would be life itself.

After Ann had been at The Clinic for one month, her treatment could be considered to be going well—after all, she was still alive. The first month is usually a "honeymoon period" of acclimation, a time to become familiar with the house, the routine, and the people with whom the patient will be living.

She kept herself frantically busy. On the unit, she fit herself into a routine of chores, vacuuming, and scrubbing floors. Her tiny hands became chafed and flaming red, with callouses as hard as a camel's hump, her knuckles cracked and bled white from the hot dishwater. She hurriedly moved furniture from room to room, like a set designer in a Broadway play. And it wasn't unusual for her to complete other patients' work before they awoke in the morning. Then she would top it all off with hours of yoga. All this energy was fueled by tiny bites of ice cream and sips of diet soda. Her weight was down to sixty-two pounds. She remained unapproachable; she went through her paces like the bewitched sorcerer's apprentice. Intensely nervous, as tightly wound as a fiddle string, she pushed people away. When people tried to hug her, she screeched; the sounds she made could have come from the monkey house at the zoo.

She was entranced by watching other patients being held and rocked as they digested bottles of warm milk, but instead of incorporating this experience, she reverted to even more cleaning, more yoga, and more long bike rides. And a new habit made its appearance: ritualistic hand washing.

I confronted her one day. "I can't understand it. Trying to engage you in conversation is as bad as getting a miser to contribute to charity."

"Anorectics are doers," she answered. "I really have no time for idle chatter."

"Everybody knows that talking about one's feelings is the most important part of therapy," I countered.

Her only reply was a quick withdrawal to another room and the whirl of the vacuum cleaner.

In time, she became unable to sleep.

The cycle of suffering had to be broken—but how? Over and over she had ridiculed psychological interpretations; this is not uncommon among bingers and starvers. Among these patients, the struggle with therapy always creates overwhelming anxiety and retreat; therefore, little gain is produced from the therapeutic endeavor.

Ann had philosophized an awareness of eating disorders sufficiently well to lecture on the subject. But, as with other young women clever in their ability to purge, her lifestyle so resisted intrusion that she was as recalcitrant as the antisocial criminal. Bitterness and defiance left little opening.

About this time, I began to hear an inner alarm, a feathery strumming in the pit of my abdomen. Over dinner one evening, I asked my wife if she remembered the Denver conference on INSIGHT. A group of analysts had held forth on their belief that a patient had to understand the unconscious meaning of his or her behavior for a positive corrective experience to take place. Following that exchange, a man had stood up and said, "Bullshit. It is the relationship that is essential; what is talked about is less important than the way it is talked about."

"Hell," I said to my wife, "I'm going to feed her something, let's say hard-boiled eggs." I intended to use simple, concrete compulsion and food to fight a nonsensical, meaningless, unreasonable paradox: a trick against a trick. "Wish me luck!" I said.

"I think you're nuts," my wife answered.

I left my dinner half eaten and drove through the dark night to Ann's unit. Standing beneath her bedroom window, the former loading platform for the parade of foodstuffs sent from mother to daughter, I wondered why I had not been sensitive to the drama as it unfolded before me; why had I failed to recognize a mother's desperation to save her daughter's life? Now it was too late, because Ann would accept nothing from her mother.

I heard a soft whimper coming from inside the bedroom, and the words, repeated over and over, "Oh God, I'm going to die, I'm going to die!"

Immediate action was needed; the next morning might be too late. I knocked twice at the front door of the cottage. There was no answer. I entered the front door. "Where the hell is everybody?" I shouted. My loud voice brought everyone, including Ann, from their beds into the living room. At my request, Ann sat next to me on the sofa.

Fifteen people waited quietly, attentively, for my next move, as though they were sitting in the front row of a movie theater. They were obviously wondering why on earth a doctor would be gathering everyone in their living room this late at night.

"Please get me a glass of cold milk," I asked one of the patients.

When the request was granted, I took several sips of milk and placed the glass on the lamp table. Then I slowly reached into my pants pocket for my red-handled Swiss army knife, snapped open its four-inch blade, grasped the quivering Ann by the hair, laid her across my knee, and moved the shiny but blunt wrong side of the blade slowly across her throat.

"I'm going to slit your throat until all the blood gushes out, kill you, if you *don't eat now!*"

I heard a sound like the gurgling of soapy water going down the drain. And a soft "No, no, please."

"Drink this milk *now!*" I shouted.

She held the glass in her bony hands and emptied it down her throat. A pause followed, then a deep breath, then tears. And more tears.

As I sat with two patients draped around one extended arm and Ann under my other arm, she drank her second glass of milk. With that second glass I felt instant relief, for I knew she would be safe until morning.

On my way home I drove past the town cemetery, continued two blocks further to the Catholic church, and entered. I am not a Catholic, and I had entered the church in the past only for weddings and funerals. But once inside, I walked to a darkened side chapel, lit a candle in the shadows, knelt, and sat in silence with clasped hands and bowed head. After a while I went on home. It was nearly midnight and I knew I needed sleep in preparation for the next day's ordeal.

Early the next morning, I phoned the unit. "She is really frightened that you will kill her today," the female houseparent said. "I can feel her defiance mobilizing for the battle. One good thing, though: she's stopped the whimpering. I think she no longer believes she will die in some ethereal way."

On the way over to the unit, I resolved to mobilize my energies and pursue the sickness, for it appeared to be in retreat (or was I fooling myself?).

I burst through the front door. "I had a vision last night," I said to Ann, who studied me with widened eyes. "I saw in that vision a sure cure to your misery."

She looked at me tenuously. "What are you talking about?"

"Hard-boiled eggs! Eggs for breakfast! Now! What time is it?" I glared dramatically at my watch. "Eight o'clock. Go into the kitchen and boil up one egg right now. Seven minutes. Tomorrow, it'll be two eggs, then three, then four. In six months, when you hit a dozen a day, you'll be cured. Isn't that wonderful!"

Ann retorted with the velocity of a racehorse, "I *hate* eggs! Adele Davis hates eggs! You're supposed to be a physician, don't you know anything about cholesterol? My mother only eats fertile eggs raw, anyway."

"Adele Davis? I think she's terrific. She starts babies on soft boiled eggs at six months, lots of iron, don't you know? *She loves eggs!* Go in there and boil one egg up right now. Ten minutes, seven to boil the egg, and three to kill the fuzzy wuzzies. Hurry up. I don't have all day."

"No! You can't make me eat eggs," Ann insisted, posturing like a stick figure made from pipe cleaners.

"Besides, I already had breakfast," she added. "Water and two tablespoons of Breyer's vanilla. I'm full. I'll burst. I'll get fat." She whined on in a singsong voice. "You're just jealous because you're lumpish. I don't need a potbelly to feel good. There was a time when I would feel hungry, but not anymore. People like you are plain riffraff. You don't know the first thing about discipline."

The bantering battle continued for one hour. "That's it," I finally said. "No more bike riding. You'll stay in the house. No more fun, just work. Not just eighteen hours a day, either, but thirty-six."

"You crazy man," she mewed. "I can't work thirty-six hours a day. There's only twenty-four hours in a day, everybody knows that."

But I left written orders with the houseparents, and I knew they would carry through on those orders: one hard-boiled egg today, and two tomorrow.

Why hard-boiled eggs? Was their consumption recommended in the literature under therapeutic interventions? Hardly. In the treatment of the anorexia-bulimia syndrome, good results are reported with all kinds of analytic and behavioral therapies, including the twelve-step program for alcoholics, and, of course, medication.

To fight over hard-boiled eggs had never been tried (or so my research indicated). Obviously, it represented a superficial cover. If a treatment is to work and have lasting results (the recidivism rate for behavioral and cognitive interventions with eating disorders is high), the patient needs to take in something supportive and filling, something emotional, from the treatment, something inside that will sustain growth while meeting daily crises. The following day I delayed my visit to the unit until well past breakfast, in the hope that Ann would eat on her own. It was quiet when I arrived. After glancing around the living room, I saw her standing inside the door frame, hands poised on hips like a professional wrestler. No longer did she have the appearance of a person waiting to die; bold resistance had replaced fear. Now she was fighting for her life, all right, but it was I she saw as her oppressor, her tormentor. Had I unknowingly replaced the sickness as the enemy? If so, we were no longer allies in a noble struggle. What now? Should I retreat? And if I did, what then?

"Did you eat those two eggs?" I asked her.

"No, I only ate one hard-boiled egg yesterday and one today. My stomach won't hold two eggs. You are a charlatan. You aren't a psychiatrist. You're the devil. How come you never talk about Freud?"

"Why? I'll tell you why. You hate Freud. You think Freud was a jerk. Anyway, I love Freud too much to allow you to belittle him. He was a kindly old grandpa to me and if you don't start eating more eggs, your brain will dry up. No wonder you're a midget. Eggs make a person strong."

"I'm not a midget. I'm small for my age, I know, but I'm not a midget."

"Sixteen years old, and no periods yet. I don't think you even know how to masturbate."

That comment brought forth a burst of tears. Ann buried her head in the female houseparent's bosom. Seeing those tears and hearing her sobs caused me to feel the sympathy and empathy one might feel toward a sick or weakened daughter. "Maybe you should have a woman therapist, maybe I'm too tough on you," I offered.

"I had a female therapist. It didn't change things."

"You probably think that only white middle-class girls get this way. Hell, I've seen it in boys—men, even. I've seen it in college girls in Nigeria fresh out of the small tribal villages."

Her compulsions continued: the cleaning, the hand washing, the yoga, day after day, Yet at times it was different. Once in a while, when someone she felt close to spoke gently, she would stop cleaning, or even delay the yoga. And it was reported that her face would soften, but only after I had departed.

In the sessions, she continued to resist the eating of eggs. "Food makes me sick," she would say. "Your food, your eggs, disagree with me." But I wondered why she, the bulimic, never vomited the eggs.

I began to take the war closer to her vulnerability. As I fought defiantly against the symptoms of the sickness, Ann was quietly allowing the houseparents to care for and protect her. That wasn't difficult, since she was starved for love.

But I did not believe the battle was over. On some days she ate three eggs; on others, four. On some days she stubbornly announced, "I'll poach them."

But the seven pounds she gained as a result of these feedings began to frighten her. After a weigh-in, she stopped eating, seeming to mobilize for one last, desperate stand.

Two months passed, and she weighed eighty pounds. Outwardly flooded with terror, she nevertheless was secretly seen to pat her stomach. But the biggest showdown, her all-out "Battle of the Bulge," was taking shape.

One morning at three, a bad dream awoke me from a sound sleep. In a cold sweat, I sat up and reviewed the dream. I was about seven or eight and was sitting at the kitchen table. Each day I would walk home the three blocks from grammar school to eat a hot lunch that my mother prepared. She firmly believed in healthy, nutritious eating. But I hated having to leave my friends, and I never ceased to admire the wonderful sandwiches of cold cuts of ham and cheese, with gobs of mayonnaise on Wonder Bread, that they brought to school.

In the dream, my mother placed a tumbler of muddy, gritty water in front of me, the effluence from the spinach to be served at dinner. When I refused to eat it, my mother angrily retorted: "Drink it down or I will make sure you are eaten by a dragon."

Had I been too harsh in my treatment of Ann? Too unyielding, too aggressive? I had begun to lose sleep, even to fret and obsess over my manner of treatment. I rationalized that the patient was improving, but I still feared the phone would ring telling me that she had worsened, or even killed herself.

After the dream, I asked myself over and over if I should phone the unit. I decided against the call. I later learned that Ann had placed a clandestine collect phone call to her mother at ten that night.

Her conversation? In a whimpering voice she had said, "Mom, they're starving me here. I'm down to fifty-nine pounds. Please help me." Then she softly laid down the receiver and stole back into the kitchen.

The phone call, of course, was a blatant lie intended to alarm her mother.

About one in the morning, a car with its headlights off moved slowly toward the back of the cottage, stopping opposite Ann's window. Cynthia Trumbull was behind the wheel. It had snowed lightly earlier in the evening. In the silent aftermath of that snow and under cover of the moonless night, Cynthia peered around the quad to see the night nurse walking out of her sight and into another cottage. She stopped at Ann's window.

"Ann, darling, here I am," she whispered. Her daughter had been waiting expectantly to hear her voice. With three cranks she opened the window. Like longshoremen unloading a ship, they shoved into the room a cache of grains, stone-ground bread, nonchemically preserved canned vegetables and meats, dried fruits, a dozen fertile eggs, two containers of raw milk, and a package of organic hot dogs.

Ann jammed everything under the bed and covered her hoard with a blue bathrobe. For two weeks, this noble

ritual of mother-daughter union against a cruel world, this
symbolic act of rescue and loyalty, flourished. The late
night rendezvous that had kept the daily battles over eggs in
open warfare remained—that is, until the stench of rotten
cheese and maggoty meat sabotaged the action.

Ann really knew that eating twelve eggs would
overload her small frame, and that I would compromise at
six if she would. She made the first move.

"Oh, yes you will!" I said in a commanding tone.
Then, more conciliatory, I amended my words.

"What? You want me to eat six! Never! Never!"
Holding herself like Mussolini, with arms folded and chin
jutting forward and upward, she encircled the room.

"Come on, you're nearly there. Six. Then six more.
Please. Do it for me?"

"No, you're a fool. You're a complete nut. You're a
mother-hater and a total fake."

"Okay, if that's the way you want it." I looked at
the female houseparent. "Linda, make twelve hard-boiled
eggs right now. I'm going to *force-feed* this girl to eat one
dozen eggs, *force* her into sanity."

Linda strode into the kitchen, talking loudly as she
prepared the eggs. "Okay, Al, one, two, three, four, six,
eight, ten, twelve. Twelve eggs are on the stove, boiling.
Coming up in ten minutes."

After a long silence, interrupted by the bubbling of
the boiling eggs, I heard deep, convulsive sobbing coming
from the far corner of the living room. Ann's entire body
was twisted in primitive sorrow. Then she fell to the floor,
rounded herself in the fetal position, and began to heave and
cry steadily. The house assistants and I picked her up and
carried her to the couch.

She continued to sob and grabbed my hand so
tightly that our hands seemed to flow into one another.

"Please, Al, I give in. Don't hurt me. I surrender."
This marked the turning point in Ann's therapy. Not that
her life was suddenly remade in a puff of magic,. Nor that a
transformation, an awakening, had taken place. Nor that she
crept out of a large leathery shell into the sunshine. Nothing
so blatant, so glaring, so magical happens in psychotherapy.
Even before that day, little changes had been taking place.
Nobody will give up a way of life needed for survival in

exchange for a future of promises. Nor for a dozen eggs.
Letting go of the sickness happens a little at a time.
Something must be taken in, tried on to see if it fits. This
turning point—though it seemed more like four
years—occurred only four months after her transfer from
the New York hospital.

3. A Transfusion of Feeling

The positive changes steadily continued. Ann thrived within
the protection of the houseparents. It wasn't long before
she wanted to pursue her education. She began home-
bound instruction in biology and algebra with a science
teacher from the local high school, who came to the cottage
two afternoons a week after school hours.

She was doggedly determined to pass her high
school equivalency examination. As she became stronger
she was able to attend classes at the high school two
mornings a week. She traveled to the SPCA, where she
found a starved, abandoned calico kitten with deformed
front paws and undeveloped teeth. She named her new
friend Appetite. (Would the two merge as one big appetite?)

I had given Ann sodium amytal (truth serum) on
several occasions, hoping to discover what lay beneath the
rigid compulsions. During the first amytal session, she
confessed that receiving anything from her mother made her
feel obligated to care fully for her mother who, she believed,
was weak and incapable of standing alone.

During the second interview, she remembered the
baby years of James, her brother. His difficulties had taken
up much of her parents' attention. A woman hired to help
her mother left for her home in Ireland; Ann responded to
this loss with an abrupt stoppage of eating. Ann
remembered this event as the beginning of her anorexia.
Also, her mother suffered a postpartum depression after the
brother's birth and was too debilitated to shield Ann from
her father's carping attacks.

Back to the psychotherapy, which was about to
change. Ann now insisted on seeing me alone rather than in
group sessions. It was during these new sessions that she

questioned and then challenged her upbringing.

"As a child," she said, "I felt that my mother was poisoning my food, and that both my parents would run off while I slept at night. My idea of a body image became confused. My father always complained that I didn't get enough exercise, and that my mother was too fat, which she really wasn't, and that she ate too much. I couldn't compete in music, sports, or studies, so I chose to divert my energy into competing in certain areas, by eating less, exercising more."

During these sessions Ann would say that her compulsions were all that mattered. Time meant nothing, and people were unreal except as obstacles to acting out her compulsions. "My starvation regimentation was everything," she remarked, "and I trusted no one. Mine was the only truth. But even at the age of three, I was in a turmoil, having inner arguments between right and wrong, wondering who liked me [she never used the term *love*] and who wanted to hurt me."

When discussing bulimia she said, "When I would vomit, I would become totally dejected, fated to die of electrolyte imbalance. Crazy, crazy, the anxiety and confusion made me crave food. I feared fatness and a swollen stomach. I would upchuck. Relief! Guilt then gone, I would feel better."

Ann had become, in her words, a robot. She said, "I had reached the top of the mountain, and I had so much control, I was out of control. Nobody could tell how insane I had become, a total slave to an inner voice."

In discussing her family life, she faced the undercurrents of her unhappiness. "Our family was well mannered and nonexpressive, yet they battled often and verbally. I had to take my father's side, or explain my mother's side to him. And my mother constantly criticized my friends. She said they weren't good enough. To her, I had been a perfect baby. If I was so perfect, why was I so miserable?"

As she became stronger, Ann began to harbor suspicions about both parents. "To my father, my mother was inferior. And he undermined anything I found interesting and attractive—my art, womanhood. Both parents undervalued me. If my drawings or art work weren't praised to the skies by both of them, I believed myself to be a failure and totally unloved."

She went on. "Actually, I was never pushed. But my father would make suggestions, emphasize my innate talents. I had to be wonderful, a superkid, always doing what I thought they wanted me to do. Underneath, I felt helpless, ineffective, confused, responsible for my father's sad, angry face. He was always angry at my mother."

Over the course of her treatment Ann began to question her mother's values and how they related to her own. In time, she linked her mother's obsession with health foods to her own disdain for eating. At those moments, she sympathized with her father.

Ann began inviting her brother to sleep over at the unit several days at a time. "I want to show him good values, what is important in life. I believe I've learned that here."

Around this time she began weekend home visits. After the seventh month of inpatient treatment, she traveled by train to visit a girlfriend in Boston. About the same time, she turned down her mother's invitation to accompany her to the Caribbean.

Around the ninth month, her whining stopped completely. Her cottage family noticed a new assertiveness which became exaggerated into a need to dominate. "I have to stop myself from taking over the groups," she said, "art, dance, music. I know it's annoying to some of the more confused patients when I follow them around. But I'm only trying to teach them to do their chores better."

She argued continually and explained it by saying, "I'm practicing for the battle with my father. You know how dogmatic he is."

She developed a skill in pottery. Later she requested her violin and, with some other patients, she formed a band that played country music at the weekly clinic dances.

She now weighed 105 pounds. No longer was she absorbed in strenuous calisthenics and yoga. Now, with other patients, she spent hours bicycling through the countryside.

In the sanctuary of her private sessions, Ann joked about eggs. But with her housemates she was all business as, with great gravity, she poached or scrambled two or three eggs for breakfast.

After one year she moved to a halfway house in the neighboring town. Each morning she met the train to The Clinic for her volunteer work with a schizophrenic boy. At the fifteenth month, she took on her first paying job—pumping gas on weekends at a filling station. "I need to find out what the real world is all about," she reasoned.

Ann's menstrual periods were erratic, the flow sparse. A gynecologist discovered that her womb was infantile, probably the result of delayed hormonal development. When hormonal injections produced no change, she became more and more depressed, thinking she would not be able to have children of her own. Afraid that the compulsions would return in greater power, she reentered the clinic to work on strengthening her sense of self.

"I don't want to lose what I've built," she said at one point. "You might say I'm going back to the well for a fresh drink."

In three months she felt renewed, and she returned to the halfway house to assume work as a paid family assistant on eight-hour rotating shifts.

She then began a relationship with a fellow worker, moving into his apartment. Six months later she and her lover moved west. She wrote that she had entered nursing school there, and that she had formed an anorexia-bulimia support group. She went to college. After receiving an R.N. she began to work as part of a surgical operating-room team. On her yearly visits home, she always found her way back to visit her friends at The Clinic.

Some questions remain unanswered. Why did Ann respond positively to a treatment that spoke only of hard-boiled eggs? Many therapists believe that the treatment focus should be on problems and conflicts, not eating. But in Ann's case, the focus was completely on eating. Once her illness was almost gone, she did feel freer to confide in me. Was there an unspoken language of mutuality in operation that replaced a need for psychologic insight?

At one time it was believed that "making the unconscious conscious" would execute change in a person. If the therapist made the "appropriate interpretation," it would lead to a conscious grasp of unconscious conflicts. Like the discovery of secrets of the East, the insight gained would make the patient well.

Instead of this ideal resolution, what resulted, more often than not, was a contingent of emotionally crippled people, thoroughly bathed in psychoanalytic theory, unhappy, and unable to negotiate daily living. Many wafted along on a thin string of existence. Psychiatry reacted by employing the opposite tack—learn by doing, and only then explore the past and speculate why. This was precisely the approach taken with Ann. Our tools were suggestion, persuasion, and counterconditioning. We would wear down bad habits that were life-killing.

Where did hard-boiled eggs fit into the scheme? Hard-boiled eggs became a hippopotamic paradox, an immense trick used against her tricks. A way to boil down the morbidity of her predicament, hoping it would disappear—and it worked! But why? 24

For Ann to let go, to replace death with a nurturing life force and uncover the will to live that lay within her, she must have felt safe within the holding environment—the surrogate family home— and with me as her therapist. As she became stronger, she met her therapist one to one with comfort and gain.

Some researchers have said that, in addition to a conceptual view of man, the most effective interpretations arise from a therapist's empathic contact with the patient, the therapist's intuitive grasp of timing, and the therapist's noninvolvement in the crazy conflicts of the patient.

Still others conclude that what is therapeutic is simply the patient's contact with someone who offers him or her an unintegrated, functional view of life; it doesn't really matter what that view is, or whether it is right or wrong.

My teacher, Theodore Reik, told me that therapy must impact with emotion, that honest insight must include feeling, not head games.

It has been fifteen years since I last saw Ann. Except for that short voluntary readmission, there has been no return of the illness. As I have thought about this case, several phenomena have become clear. The active treatment of emotional and mental disorders has undergone drastic changes during this time, many of them due to the following events:

1) The elimination of large government hospitals (a cost-reducing movement first started in Italy).

2) Shifts from private doctor-to-patient relationships to the introduction of a third partner, the case manager, and managed care, resulting in prescribed lengths of hospital stays, fee schedules, and unified standards of care (so that, for example, not using medication might be considered malpractice).

Most often, determinations are made in an office thousands of miles away, and only by the review of records—not by an on-sight consultation with patients and their treating doctors. This practice is a two-edged sword. No doubt it has unified a standard of care, with improvement in many situations. But it places suspicion on experimentation and exploration.

Obviously, to treat bulimic anorexia nervosa with a dialogue of hard-boiled eggs would exceed any recognized standards. And it would be difficult to find references for such a treatment in any recognized textbook.

Hypothetically, I could be hauled into court to defend my practices. What would I say in my defense? Did I have license to try a new approach because the patient was considered untreatable, the prognosis pessimistic, the danger of death more than remote? Perhaps I would be able to hide behind the wide skirts of the American Board of Examiners in Psychodrama, Sociometry and Group Psychotherapy, for the techniques could be seen as "role playing."

Then again, there are differences. Was the use of irony and ridicule, faced with the seriousness of Ann's condition, an act of bravery or of foolishness? Perhaps it worked by enabling her, like many who have felt fear during wartime, to overcome that fear by imitating a more daring comrade.

Also, I used the Hansel and Gretel fable to advantage. Every suffering child, at some time, experiences his or her parents as cruel and unloving, and yearns in dreams for the perfect, all-loving family. I paradoxically assumed the role of the cruel and uncaring parent, thus absorbing the patient's negativity and freeing her recalcitrance. Thus she made the positive changes she was opposed to making.

Furthermore, by utilizing the outrageous and the unpredictable, I did not allow the patient any time to organize a rigid defense. Intrusion was continuous and emotion-arousing. And she was always treated with dignity, never with patronage; the interaction was between two human beings.

Every day she received a continuous transfusion of healthy emotion within the confines of a safe and supportive family unit, a psychiatric incubator.

Lastly, most patients say that whatever strength, self-understanding, and change of attitude they achieve in therapy comes about through their own efforts. The bottom line is, "I did it all myself!"

About a year ago, one of Ann's fellow workers at The Clinic, who had been her roommate when both were patients, mentioned that Ann had broken off her relationship with her former lover and had started a new one. Furthermore, Ann was pregnant. Not too many months later, I received a letter:

> Wonderful to hear from you. My baby boy is growing fast. He's one month old, with reddish hair. We named him Nathaniel Aaron Jamison (his dad is Jonah L. Jamison). Jonah and I are new at being parents, but we are very glad to have Nathaniel in our lives.
>
> I met Jonah about two years ago when he was visiting Tucson from Connecticut. He is the best partner and friend I ever had. I'm still doing nursing (on leave for another month, then back to work). It's very hard to make ends meet in Tucson. Salaries are low and cost of living high. We may move soon in order to provide us with more income. Tucson has been a wonderful home to me, but it's gradually losing charm and becoming a high-income tourist trap, and millionaire estates are cropping up everywhere.

Both Jonah and I are musicians, playing bluegrass and old-time swing music professionally.

I have become a good enough fiddle/violin player to be hired as a local studio musician every so often.

I have heard that you are still working, have not retired or given it all up. I know many who have. Health care is a disaster in our country. I currently cannot afford health insurance, and am trying to find a way to buy coverage for my son. We were able to use Medicaid for my delivery and the baby for six months, thank goodness. As a nurse, I get to see many "indigent" patients who use the medical service that cost millions when they are on respirators for all the time they need. I am proud to work for a hospital that treats people, regardless of ability to pay. I love my job with its components of psychology, spirit, science, and technology. It feeds all the aspects of me (except music).

I've enclosed some pictures of our new family. My folks are proud to be grandparents, at last. Take care of yourself,

Much love,

Ann

P.S. My son loves hard-boiled eggs. He eats them mashed.

Chapter II
Deep Water

1. Death and Transfiguration

There is that occasional patient who, knowingly or not, will test the moral fiber of a physician. When this occurs, the physician is compelled to brush to a new sheen an existing inner code that has possibly become dulled by inattention.

This second story describes such a patient. It all began in early spring at the University of Texas at Austin. Dorm lights blazed as students crammed for midterms, but most of the rooms darkened by midnight as young voices, with nervous laughter and words of despair reflecting the rigors of academic life, faded away to end another day.

It was a different picture inside room 302, with flickering candlelight instead of harsh fluorescent lamps and impassioned poetry reading, accompanied by pill popping and wine swigging, instead of frantic studying. The clock struck two. Two young women sat cross-legged on the bed and read aloud to each other from the writings of Sylvia Plath.

"Cheryl, listen to this," said Gail. "It's called 'Lesbos,'" and she began to read, the fluorescent light wincing off and on like a terrible migraine.

> And my child—look at her, face down on the floor!
> Little unstrung puppet, kicking to disappear!
> Why, she is a schizophrenic,
> I should sit on a rock off Cornwall and comb my hair.
> I should wear tiger pants. I should have an affair.
> We should meet in another life, we should meet in

the air,
Me and you.

These ritualistic candlelight readings had been going on for a month. The young women had quit the swimming team and scorned their friends until they had only each other for companionship. Neither one had opened a textbook for six weeks. Gail had not attended class for two weeks, and Cheryl had stopped just four days prior to this evening. Gail had even refused to leave the room for two days, depending on Cheryl to bring her food from the dining room.

After a thick silence, Gail said, "You know, Cheryl, I hate my parents. They don't give a damn at all."

Cheryl's only response was, "I feel horrible."

Gail waited a moment, then began again to read in monotone:

I'm doped and thick from my last sleeping pill.
The smog of cooking; the smog of hell
Floats our heads, two venomous opposites.
I call you Orphan, orphan. You are ill.

It was nearly three, and Gail's head was beginning to bob forward. Cheryl, annoyed, shook her shoulders. "C'mon, let's finish this poem."

Gail, in a daze, began to read again. When she finished, Cheryl giggled, swallowed another small red pill, and washed it down with a glass of Gallo Red.

When Gail began to doze off again, Cheryl leaned forward and shook her gently. "Gail, come on, let's finish up. You've got to get me up at eight o'clock. I told Nell I'd see her for one final session."

Gail slapped her ears to prove her she was awake, and softly read on:

Now I am silent, hate
Up to my neck,
Thick, thick.
I do not speak.
I say I may be back
You know what lies are for!

Even in your Zen Heaven we shan't meet.

"She wrote that in 1962," Cheryl said, "one year before she died. I even know the date she did it. February 11, 1963." After a moment's silence she added, "You still seeing your shrink?"

Gail's tone became venomous. "That creep! I gave up on him. He keeps bawling me out, telling me I have talent but I'm not doing anything with it. You know, the same stuff he always says: 'Southwestern breaststroke champion! Southwestern butterfly champion! From a good family! Pull yourself together and show some guts! He'll see, they'll all see.'"

The young women had spent the Christmas recess with Gail's family, the Adamses, at Fort Myers on the Florida Gulf. Cheryl had looked forward to sunning on the beach, absorbing the quiet. It had promised to be a perfect escape from her own parents and their incessant talk about divorce. Cheryl's mother, anxious and always depressed, repeatedly phoned her at school, always wanting her support against Cheryl's father. But Cheryl had nothing more of herself to give.

Often remarking on her friend's lack of animation, Cheryl had persuaded Gail to seek therapy at the Student Health Clinic. Cheryl herself had started to see Nell Baker, a young student psychologist. Once in the presence of the Adamses, Cheryl understood why Gail exhibited such low spontaneity. The family displayed unimpeachable courtesy toward one another. Each person was immaculately clean and extremely proper on the beach. The household was orderly, unblemished—and dead.

As New Year's Eve approached, Cheryl could no longer tolerate the Adamses. "Let's get back to school, Gail," she had said one day. "It's just not working here." Gail had agreed, indifferently.

The Adamses had not questioned their early departure, which only added to Cheryl's despondency. Her friend's family was uncaring, and her own family was dysfunctional.

Now, in the early morning hours, they read from "Two Views of a Cadaver Room."

Dying is not like everything else.
I do it exceptionally well.
 I do it so it feels like Hell.
I do it so it feels real.
I guess you could say I've got a call.

Gail reached across to touch Cheryl's leg but Cheryl flinched. "You know I don't like to be touched, Gail. It's nothing personal, you understand."

They took turns reading. They were totally lost in the poetry, in each other, in the Seconal, and in the wash of wine.

At four o'clock, Cheryl wavered. "Jesus, I have an appointment with Nell at eight o'clock."

"Why the hell are you still seeing that shrink?" Gail asked. "What's she ever done for you, anyway?"

Cheryl knew that Gail had become more despondent because of her own psychiatrist's flippant attitude. But Nell cared for Cheryl, and they had established a relationship.

At Cheryl's silence, Gail withdrew into herself, obviously resentful that Cheryl shared her secrets with someone else.

"You know," Gail finally muttered, "at the last session, that bastard shrink really let loose, yelled at me. 'Look at you, solid Olympic material, sexy woman. Where the hell are your guts?'" Her fists were clenched. "Can you imagine? Know what? I'll just show him where my guts are."

Embracing a small bottle of Seconal, she spilled the pills on the bed and counted them—thirty, forty, forty-five.

"Here, Cheryl, let's divvy them up. Twenty for you and twenty-five for me. Beautiful love sleep...and when we awake, we'll be at peace together. Won't it be wonderful?"

She poured herself another glass of wine, then handed the bottle to Cheryl. With the gestures of a Juliet, Gail swallowed the pills, one by one, with intermittent gulps of the wine. And Cheryl, in her adulating mimicry, did the same.

By five o'clock the candlelight had waned. In the trees outside the window, a flock of guinea hens cackled in the dawn. But in Room 302, all was quiet.

At eight o'clock Cheryl failed to show for her appointment
with Nell. As the clock ticked the minutes away, Nell grew
concerned and phoned the university hospital emergency
room. She expressed her concern to the physician who had
given Cheryl her medication, but he reassured her; she had
come in the previous day for a refill and had been in good
spirits. She said she felt better, with no suicidal thoughts,
and wanted to continue the pills to ensure she didn't slip
back. She probably had forgotten her appointment because
of midterm exams.

On the following morning at nine-thirty, Mary Ellen
Saunders, Cheryl's backstroke partner, walked up three
flights of stairs. She hoped to convince Cheryl to rejoin the
team.

Reaching the door, she knocked once, twice, then
listened to what sounded like soft moans coming from
inside. "Cheryl! Gail! Are you in there?"

No answer.

She ran to a phone and dialed Student Health. When
the on-call doctor answered, she cried out, "I swear I hear
sounds in Room 302, but nobody answers my knock. I just
feel something bad has happened."

The doctor and his assistant arrived at the scene and
broke down the door. Mary Ellen shrieked at the sight. In
the bed nearest the window lay the ashen-faced body of a
young woman. In the other bed, another woman lay in a
fetal position. The stench of urine and feces was sickening.

Covering his mouth and nose with a handkerchief,
the doctor felt the second woman's jugular and carotid
pulse. After instructing Mary Ellen to call an ambulance, he
injected this woman with a stimulant, then began mouth-to-
mouth resuscitation.

In the hospital Cheryl Henderson lingered between
life and death for nine days, five of which she spent in a
deep coma, accompanied by respiratory failure and
pneumonia. With the return of corneal reflexes, physical
recovery came quickly.

Once awake, Cheryl inquired about Gail. Learning
that her friend was dead, she slipped into silence. She began
to follow an unvaried routine of a single walk along the

hallway and a vigil at the sixth-floor window. Fear of another suicide attempt—either by jumping from the window ledge or hanging from a bed sheet—prompted her therapist to call The Clinic.

I listened to a brief rundown of events. "Please have her parents accompany her."

Big Jim Henderson was a man behind the scenes of Texas politics. He sat across from me, thumpingly elephantine, flanked by Cheryl and his wife, Emma.

"I want you to know," he said, pointing his finger for emphasis, "that us Hendersons don't come from just ordinary stock. Cheryl's great-great-great-grandfather was governor; he beat Sam Houston, he did. I don't know about my little girl, though. She's the baby, you know, youngest of three. She's got hundreds of medals for swimming meets. And whole rooms full of trophies. Champ in high school. Goes over to Austin, becomes Olympic material, and then quits the team. Tell me, Doc, is she sick or just plain mean?"

Cheryl sat in silence, probably hallucinating. When I didn't answer, he went on. "When she was still in diapers, I'd say, 'Now, Cheryl, you go over there and eat those string beans.' Well, she'd take those beans and put them in her ears or down her diaper until her plate was empty. And could she hold her breath in a temper! Tell me what's that all about, huh, Doc?

"And one more thing. I don't think it's good for her to be around her mother. Her mother's taken every damn pill in the books, and her closet is still full. When they're together, it's no good."

When her father stopped talking, Cheryl rose, with a sudden resolute look to her face and eyes. She pointed her finger at him and shouted, "I hate that man right there. I hate him."

Emma Henderson, thin and heavily made up, spoke in a strong drawl. "I guess I've been too weak to give Cheryl what she needed or to stand up to her father. I'll tell you one thing, though. She's the kindest of the girls. My other two daughters—the oldest is married—pay no attention to me, never have. Cheryl has always been kind to me, and has always listened to my problems."

I soon learned a few cogent facts about Cheryl. She

had indiscriminately swallowed items from her mother's medicine cabinet and had spent what would have been her senior year of high school as an inpatient where her mother had been a patient years earlier. The doctors at this hospital had characterized this incident as a cry for help rather than attempted suicide. Their therapy focused on her "immaturity and misinterpretation of people."

Her depression lingered and treatment continued. Much later, Cheryl would say the treatment might have helped, but it was a romance with a young male patient that ended her stay and allowed her to return home and complete high school.

At The Clinic, the initial treatment plan would center on her severe depression and the likelihood of another suicide attempt. No new medicine would be prescribed.

Tests showed her liver was working overtime to cleanse her body from her latest ingestion. A recently recovered female patient would remain with her; because of this patient's own experiences, she could interpret Cheryl's feelings, and she would act as a positive force against Cheryl's smoldering negativity. A married couple, serving as houseparents, lived in the cottage along with several other patients.

Though Cheryl tried to adjust to her new surroundings, most of the time she withered in bed, holding herself in a knee-to-chest position, rocking and humming. Despising small talk, she rarely entered into conversations.

On her fourth day of hospitalization, I confronted this unbearable mute scene. "What are your thoughts?" I asked.

After some hesitation, she drew her hands around her mouth and said softly, "Gail is calling me, calling me to the grave." Then she scowled and added, "It's continual. I believe I killed her. Why did I live and why did she die? She tells me it is beautiful there, and that I am a fool not to join her."

On the eighth day I walked abruptly into the unit and marched over to Cheryl, who was sitting with head bent almost into her lap. "I want to ask you a serious question, Cheryl. Does your mother really want to keep you alive, or would she prefer that you were dead?"

I searched her face for a reaction, but she remained as stiff as a stump of wood. I went on, trying for some impact.

"You want to hear what she told me over the phone? She said you were cold-blooded, calculating, and that she won't let you destroy her. She thinks you're out to get her. What's that all about?"

Tears trickled from her eyes. "I have no lungs. My soul has been ripped off. If you're smart, you'll keep away from me. People can't be around me, and I can't be touched."

I saw the tears as a sign that some slight contact had been made. I spoke gently, trying to kindle that connection. "Would you like to see me alone? Perhaps it would be easier."

"What's the difference?"

In the face of her apathy I would need all my faculties to make further contact. This was difficult in the present circumstances, with many other patients in the room constantly demanding to be the center of attention.

I later met in my office with Cheryl and her female houseparent. Cheryl sat in an armchair two feet away, head down, shoulders slumped, back hunched over, eyes closed. "How are things going?" I asked her.

"Oh, all right, sir." The soothing tone of her Southern accent seemed genuine and natural. Though pleasantly different from the harsh directness of Northerners, Southern gentility can mask emotions just as raw, tormenting, and uncivilized.

Abruptly she took on an accusing demeanor. "You betrayed my confidence. You told my mother everything. I didn't want her to know I was still suicidal. You're a liar, a fake, and a quack. You can't be trusted with anybody's secrets. I told you to keep it a secret."

Shocked by this sudden attack, I took my time to respond. "You told your houseparent the same secret and swore him to secrecy, too. Anyway, I wouldn't feel right, your telling me to keep my mouth shut and my being the only one knowing you're suicidal. You really are a case of committed suicide. You're dead by all medical and psychiatric thinking. It was only the doctors who brought you back to life."

"Bullshit. I happen to have a strong body. Anyway, it's my curse that I'm still alive."

It was important to shift emphasis away from talk of her death.

"Why don't you view a movie that was made here. It's called *Other Voices*. Many patients are in it, but the one who might get your attention is a fifteen-year-old boy who was here for a year and a half."

The movie, I explained, was a study in suicide. The boy had made significant developmental changes but they weren't enough. He hanged himself.

"So?" she said, with a mocking smile.

I ignored her challenge. "Suicide is an enigma no authority seems to understand. We had two suicides that year. Maybe it was contagious, I don't know, because there haven't been any since." I watched Cheryl carefully. "We'll probably have more, though, because we accept many patients on the edge."

The boy in the film had requested LSD. Though illegal in the 1960s, it was as easy to get on the street as it is today. The staff had rejected its use in therapy as too dangerous. Later, as I often do, I had spent hours working through that case, wondering if I had done enough, obsessing over possible errors of omission.

Death could easily win again. Cheryl's will to live was slipping, and I wanted her to know that the staff and I cared, that it mattered to us that she live.

With that uncanny perceptiveness, that sixth sense possessed by many people who wade through the deep waters of mental illness, Cheryl fixed upon my self-doubt. "I'm not interested in your troubles, shrink," she said. Then she began a rhythmic rocking. An angelic smile softened her face.

"You know, suicide is funny," I said, as her angelic gaze made me think that Gail was calling to her again. "It hits the poor, it hits the rich. It affects young kids, too, kids five and six years old.

"She looked at me for a moment, then laughed. "I hear it's highest among psychiatrists, doctor." Her words took on caustic severity. "Let me tell you something. I know people who were perfectly rational when they killed themselves." She counted on her fingers. "Aunt Lynn, my cousin Doris, Mrs. Williamson, my neighbor, and of course, Gail."

"Suicides have certain irrationalities in common," I retorted. "For one thing, they think they are better than God, and they look down on people. They all think nobody can help them, and they always think they're smarter than other people."

"I don't," she said quickly.

Ignoring her interruption, I labored on. "But to me, they're all sick. Maybe we'd have fewer killings if we left the power of life and death to God."

She dramatically drew two fingers across her throat and said, "Let me tell you a little secret, doctor. I'd kill myself right here in front of you if I didn't have a fear of rotting in eternal Hell."

To stay alive, she would have to make an earthly commitment more grounded than the fear of Hellfire. In fact, if we could clear away that self-deceptive baggage she carried, we might find a spark of attachment to life.

"The Bible doesn't condemn suicide," I said, continuing to attack her illusion. "The Jews at Masada chose mass suicide rather than Roman torture and slavery. The early Christians committed suicide to avoid earthly sin and eternal damnation. The fifth century and St. Augustine changed all that. St. Augustine called suicide a 'detestable and damnable wickedness.'"

I watched her carefully, knowing she was alive enough to continue arguing stubbornly for death.

"St. Augustine had three reasons for his pronouncement. You know what they were? One, the Sixth Commandment, 'Thou shalt not kill'; two, that suicides deprive themselves of last absolution for their sins; and, three, that suicide is a rejection of God's will."

"You know, doctor, Christ himself was a suicide. He was a martyr, but he was a suicide, too. He had to die at the hands of someone else to set an example. You would probably call that a weakness."

"Yes, I would. All martyrs are basically weak in one way. I believe it's better to set an example of how to live a full and happy life. You must have had a rotten childhood."

"Yeah, all shrinks say that. So what. It's all me. I'm

rotten to the core. It's all my fault."

I wanted to counter with, "All potential suicides say that," but I let it pass. What I did say was, "Somehow, I don't think that's true, although I understand how you feel. Not many people have experienced your traumas and persecutions. But people in the death camps had it worse."

She had stopped listening. Instead, she sat there calling out, "Gail! Gail!" Her eyes lifted toward the heavens, her arms were outstretched. "She is wonderful. She calls me and I must join her."

Looking for something to divert her thoughts, I appealed to her feeling for others. It was a stop-gap measure; I could not help her tomorrow if she killed herself that night.

"Listen, Cheryl, do me a favor, please? Don't kill yourself, at least not now. Suicide is contagious, you know? Once it starts, there's no telling where it will stop. There are several people around here on the edge, even a few staff members who aren't too strong. God knows, I'm probably not far from it myself."

I reached for her hand, holding it for a moment. She didn't pull it away. Then, without relinquishing the grip, I escorted her back to the unit.

Going over my notes later, I realized that Gail, through her suicide, had become Cheryl's exalted and beatified antilife heroine—the abused virginal martyr, the pure saint. Cheryl now felt doubly inadequate, a failure in death as well as in life. If she were to die by her own hand, it would have to be a magnificent feat. Not only would she have to duplicate Gail's triumph, she would have to surpass it.

I had encouraged her to put her feelings into words. In deep pain, she began to write notes to me. Her tone ranged from angry to sugary sweet. The handwriting varied; most often it was in small script ("as if I'm a tiny ant, that's how I feel about myself most of the time") but when she was angry, it was bold.

One day I brought one of the notes into the unit and moved to a corner of the room. Cheryl, recognizing the note as her own, followed me. We sat down and examined the written material. Somewhat hesitantly, not knowing what reaction to expect, I said, "You know, I can't tell your writing from your mother's. You write the same and sound the same. It's as if you are actually her."

There was only a slight frown from my patient.

On rare occasions a strong, determined, optimistic, clear-thinking Cheryl would emerge, and I became hopeful. Was this the Cheryl of the future? Then this free self would quickly hide behind the seething pain and suffering, the bleakness and doom, the obsession with suicide.

One day I found a note in my mailbox. "Dr. Honig, please read this poem. Gail is waiting for me, beckoning me. I know I must join her. The poem is from *Wanting To Die* by Anne Sexton.

> I have nothing against life.
> But suicides have a special language.
> Like carpenters, they want to know which tools.
> They never ask why build.

Through selected poetry, Cheryl encountered her longing for death and her failure to recognize life support. Like Anne Sexton, Cheryl knew intellectually that she was surrounded by life wherein others find joy. Yet all that remained was her passion for death.

The note alarmed me. In this poem Cheryl had found justification for her feelings. I ran to the unit, only to find her sitting in a corner. Placing one arm around her shoulder, and pressing her hand in mine, I looked into her eyes.

"Cheryl, please, I know your pain. Can't we make a pact? If we can't make a pact to live, then lets make a suicide pact—pledge ourselves together in death."

With these words I hoped to replace Gail in Cheryl's brain. If I could become as important to her as Gail, my voice calling her to life might eventually become stronger than Gail's calling her to death. It was a risk; voices (hallucinations) are devious, and it could easily become my voice she heard calling her to death.

Tears formed in Cheryl's eyes. She squeezed my hand and put her head on my chest. When finishing with patients that evening, I checked my mailbox. Another note, another poem.

O Sylvia, Sylvia,
crawl down alone
into the death I wanted so badly and for so long
the one we talked of so often each time
we downed three extra dry martinis in Boston.
the death we drank to,
the motives and then the quiet deed?

"Sylvia's Death," by Anne Sexton

She was dragging me deeper into her morbidity, but in reading the poem I felt some satisfaction, as though she had given me a highly personal gift. However, I also felt this young woman had little respect for the profession of psychiatry.

It was important that Cheryl live through one day at a time. With each day her memory of Gail would grow weaker; no new memories of their mutual symbiosis could be generated since Gail was dead. As Gail's hallucinated image became fainter and less frequent, the strong bond between them would be stretched by the passage of time until it was gone.

Although Cheryl stubbornly insisted that Gail alone drew her toward death, I began to understand there was another, perhaps stronger, force. And I, obsessed with saving her life, was involved in a deeper way. The forces of death within Cheryl had become my personal enemy. I knew I could not rest until I was certain Cheryl would live.

A break in the case came when Cheryl requested a private session. "It's the only way I get a chance to talk to you, Dr. Honig," she said. "When you're in the unit, the other patients take all your time. I know I'm not worth much, and I'm going to be dead anyway, but my father is paying for my stay here, and I don't feel he's getting his money's worth."

I believed that while Cheryl's problems had, no doubt, originated early in life, she now had lived with these symptoms for so long, they had become part of her character structure. Also, a suicidal act is performed in desperation when no other exit from a trap seems to exist. I believed that she was protecting her family, and that she had become the aggressor in this duet of death, keeping a secret from everyone. But I didn't know why.

One thing was certain. She had been admitted under emergency status to the only open bed available in a unit that already had too much patient disturbance. If she was to recover, the therapeutic nurturing had to continue along with the suicide watch. That meant she would have to be moved as soon as possible.

2. Symbiosis

At the Gottshalk cottage, Cheryl was the only female patient among six males. She continued to face each day with her head searching a narrow area of the floor and her matted hair covering her eyes. Her back rounded into her shoulders and forearms, and she carried her small hands as if they were amputated stubs.

She and her new female houseparent, Lorna, who had the patience of a Mother Theresa, quickly developed an empathic relationship. Lorna had a personal understanding of pathematic pain; she had been assaulted and raped before her marriage to Paul.

On Cheryl's first night at the cottage, Lorna offered her a bottle of warm milk to help her sleep, and bonding began immediately. Cheryl later told me it was the singular extraordinary experience of her lifetime. Like magic, the burning pain in her stomach seemed to melt away; her arms and legs felt "warm and tingly"; the tension headache disappeared; her face flushed. She soon fell asleep with no need for evening medication.

The next morning, Lorna helped her wash and dress. "Gee, maybe I won't even need the meds any longer," Cheryl remarked.

"I hope so," Lorna answered, "but let's take it one step at a time."

"Dr. Honig said I should be examining my relationship with my mother." Cheryl looked naively at Lorna as she spoke.

She was reaching out to someone else besides myself. Lorna, happy about her patient's beginning confidence, did not dare to comment, for fear of an immediate withdrawal. "What do you think about that?" was all she said.

"I don't know. I'm confused. I know I hate my father. When my mother went to the mental hospital, he beat me viciously. He told me her condition was my fault. I was only nine years old. I guess I was sort of a mean, stubborn kid."

Her eyes searched the floor, as if it were the only safe place she was permitted to explore. "My mother had shock treatments in that hospital. She's never been off pills since. Twelve years now she's been on tranquilizers. Three times I OD'd on her pills when I was in high school. They never knew it, and don't know to this day." She paused and then said, "It might help if I could sleep regularly."

"Do you sleep with anything—a doll, teddy bear, or favorite blanky?" Lorna asked, as if it were a routine question.

"Oh, I have my little teddy bear and I do take my pills. My mother takes the same pills I do. But Dr. Honig only gives me the prescribed dose. Hell, I used to swallow four or five of those at a time."

"Well," said Lorna, "if the teddy bear and the pills don't do it for you, I've got another idea. Why don't you and I make a life-size doll. If you lie down in the middle of the floor, I'll trace a pattern your size on a bed sheet. Then we can both sew it together and stuff it with old newspapers, maybe paint a human image on it, and you can sleep with it. Actually, Cheryl, it might be fun, and you can call it 'Mother,' 'Cheryl Junior,' or anything you want."

"It sounds interesting," Cheryl answered. There was a note of sadness in her voice. "I had a Raggedy Ann doll once."

Somewhat bored with her old reliables, Cheryl seemed in a mood to try something new. They began the tracing on an old sheet and finished the doll in three days.

So Cheryl had a new companion at night. She curled up with it, rolled over on it; most often she held it in her left arm, so that she could still suck her right thumb. She was sometimes even heard talking to the makeshift doll. "You stupid shithead," she said once. "I hate you!" With that, she threw it to the floor, kicking it in the head.

When she saw Lorna standing at the doorway, she was embarrassed. Tilting her head and shaking her hair over her eyes, she spoke in a babyish voice. "I'm sorry. I didn't know you were there."

"That's okay," Lorna replied. "You have to get it out." Lorna was amazed how her patient could climb the scale from infant to street urchin in the space of twenty seconds.

One day I arrived at the office building to find Cheryl curled up on the outside step in her regular fetal position. At my invitation she lifted herself slowly, and then she cautiously followed me into my office. Never the first into a room. Why? Was it a fearful remnant from her father's beatings, a need to keep everyone in sight?

"He'd line me and my two sisters up for Sunday morning prechurch inspection. His little soldiers, he called us. He checked our dresses to see if they were neat and starched, looked for spots all over our shoes, our white socks. Then he fixed our white gloves before we left."

I listened respectfully, then asked how she felt.

"Rotten. It's no use. Why do you even bother?"

She had folded her arms across her body, the soft parts hidden. Unnerved by my staring, she threw out both arms in front of her. "Okay, look see. Yes! I cut myself last night." Her attitude was defiant yet resigned. "I'm made to pay with my flesh. They demand more each time. I can't stand it much longer. Death will bring peace. Human closeness is nice but not for me. You're a human being, but I'm not. I deserve only punishment. When I try, I suffer more. I know you don't understand." Trying to distract her from morbid thoughts, I said, "Lorna told me you took a warm bottle last night, and that you two had a long talk." I tried to show compassion, to empathize, but also to penetrate deeper.

"Yes, we did. So what? Nothing will help, really. Remember the patient that was here because she stuck a bread knife through her chest and narrowly missed her heart? Well, I want to do something like that but I haven't—at least, not yet."

She paused for a moment. "I hear two voices. One is yours, saying you love me. The other tells me to cut through my chest. I'm confused because that voice is yours, too. I'm still alive, but for how long? You see how I cut myself? I'm weak. I have to fight hard not to kill you. I battle the voices that tell me not to write you notes. It's just like before Gail and I took those pills. The more I say, the more frightened I am. Eventually you'll abandon me. I think you should. I thought of starving myself, but I believe my stomach would rupture and cause me pain."

I listened for a clue but found none. A therapist hopes the patient will join in a mutual battle against irrationality that will help the patient develop human relationships. Frieda Fromm-Reichmann and John Rosen thought psychotics were capable of this, thus giving birth to the psychotherapy of schizophrenia and schizoid states. Freud had rejected this idea, refusing to treat psychosis.

But Cheryl projected no self-image. Instead, she clung to whoever was near. The dependency became so intense, the other person eventually moved not closer, but further away. I felt sure this pattern had been lifelong. Sometimes she relaxed, and could join with another in a meaningful transfer of emotion. At those times, her face softened, her body relaxed. She might project hope of one day having a boyfriend, a baby, a home—the things most women consider their birthright. Then, like the strike of lightning in a rainstorm, her mood would change.

In a wild moment, could she plunge a knife through her heart, or maybe mine? Cut the thin thread of human contact that still remained? Or had she already gone over the edge? I didn't know.

I decided to fight her illness with what she needed most from a physician—devotion, dedication, perseverance. She believed somebody wanted her dead, and I had to respect her concrete ideas. So, with trepidation, I began bearing down on the images of the past that had killed her spirit. Sometimes this works like magic, and when it does, it can make mental illness seem illusionary: here one minute, gone the next.

"Your problem is as raveled as an old ball of yarn," I said. "It would be romantic to think it all began with Gail. That isn't quite the truth. It goes back further, you don't hate your father for no reason at all." I continued on probing. "And maybe it goes even deeper. I notice that you always protect your mother. But there is obviously something dragging you down to the grave. I'm not going to say flat out that it is your mother. But I suspect there is an infectious weakness in both of you. A symbiotic union. Something outrageously destructive."

Though I tried to break into this alliance, Cheryl's depression and seething despair remained intact. She left that session, walked across the lawn to her cottage, went upstairs, and closed the door.

Later that night, she phoned her mother.

"Mom, he says you want me dead."

"I hope you don't believe it. I would kill myself this minute if I thought you did." Cheryl, of course, said she didn't believe it. "I know you love me, Mom," she was heard to say. "We all should have left that bastard [her father] long ago."

About six the next morning I awoke to a call from Lorna, who told me that Cheryl had stayed in her room all evening after the call, with the light on, humming and rocking.

After a hurried breakfast, I hastened to the cottage and began a group session with patients and staff. These meetings were held every morning, and served several functions: family unity, overnight problems, outline of the day's activities, and of course individual therapy. Seriously ill patients often find the group setting less threatening than the one-to-one.

Cheryl was not present.

As the session continued, she quietly descended the stairs and slid into a corner of the room. Lorna immediately sat on the floor next to her.

"Thanks for coming in," I said, pausing in my work with another patient.

"Yeah, yeah, yeah," she answered dispassionately.

Still looking at the patient I had been working with, I said, "You know something, Cheryl?"

She answered, "What?" She had assumed fetal position. Her hair was matted, her jeans dirty, her jersey stained (she had slept in her clothes), and she wore no shoes.

I pressed the attack. "I'm convinced your mother

wants you dead." My goal was to bring to light hidden thoughts she had been harboring yet denying.

Instantly, while a thirteen-year-old schizophrenic boy sat on folded legs and rocked, and a psychotic, urine-soaked Vietnam veteran laughed as though mocking any attempt at rationality, Cheryl dashed for the door and ran out.

People scattered as if someone had tossed a bomb into the room. But it was Cheryl that they were trying to catch up to.

It was the Woodson instructor, in his jeep, who saw a familiar barefoot young woman racing up the highway. Recognizing the jeep, she ran faster, heading directly for an overpass. She was about to leap off the bridge when a passing police officer tackled her. The Woodson instructor, the first staff member to reach her, held her by the right thigh. She rewarded both men with blows and kicks to the face. Others arrived within moments and restrained her while she kicked and screamed, "You bastards, all men are bastards."

Straightjacketed, her ankles cuffed in soft restraints, she sat next to me on the ride back to The Clinic, muttering, "I hate you all. I'm going to call my father and tell him to get me out of here. He's wasting his money, and I know he'll agree with me."

"He's already complaining about money, and the man's a multimillionaire. He never believed you were sick, just bad. Just settle down, will you, and at least let us catch our breath." I looked at my watch. Only fifteen minutes had passed since the beginning of the session.

Back in the living room where the scene had started, Cheryl again lashed out. "Doctor, there's no way in the world you can stop me from killing myself if I set my mind to it. Put me on a twenty-four-hour watch. There will be that moment when they let down their guard. That's all the time I need. I can put a rolled-up bed sheet around my neck and pull it tight, or put my fingers in an electric socket, or choke on my food, even hold my breath."

Her words reverberated through the room. They entered my head and I spit them out, feeling nothing—unimpassioned professionalism. Or so I thought. Actually, her taunts of suicide were making me lie to myself. She toyed with me by flirting with death, the archenemy of the physician. She could kill herself any time she wanted to. And she was determined not to grant me the satisfaction of saving her life.

Yes, I had choices, but none that I would enjoy. I could distance and insulate myself from her pain, or grope forward like a blind man with a cane.

Cheryl understood death perhaps more than I did. If she were to truly heal, I would have to take my own journey. I thought of D.H. Lawrence's words: "Are you willing to be made nothing? Dipped into oblivion? If not, you will never really change." I had to listen and learn to transfer myself, to become her, patiently and painfully, or she would remain alienated.

Then, once again, the unexpected happened. Cheryl, still wrapped in straightjacket and ankle restraints, asked everyone to leave the room so she could be alone with me. What was this new ploy? I asked everyone to leave.

After the room emptied, she said, "Dr. Honig—may I call you Al?—God wasn't very kind to me, I guess. I've been watching the patients here. Most hallucinate and are in another world. They're lucky because they're like zombies and, in a way, they're already dead. And who cares what happens to them? I understand why no doctors want to work here. What for? To spend their lives resurrecting the *dead?* Your colleagues think you're crazy, and they're probably right."

Once more with quixotic abandon, she began to soliloquize: "You might be right about my mother, I don't know. I remember when I was sixteen and seventeen, I spent each summer in my room.
I came out only to go to the toilet and to eat. I never bathed, and I rocked back and forth on my bed. I came out at night when the house was quiet and read books about mental illness.

"My mother talked to herself and complained about me. She stopped a school friend from visiting me. Her incessant talking freaked me out, so one day I cut off most of my hair. I swallowed thirty aspirins, told my mother, and was taken to the hospital to have my stomach pumped. I stayed in the psychiatric ward under observation for ten days, came home, and then went right back into my room."

She paused to see if I had absorbed her words. Apparently satisfied, she continued. "I fought going to the mental hospital where my mother had been. The night before I went, my father tried to strangle me, and my mother stopped him."

She spoke rapidly without emotion. "When I was a child, and played with friends, my infantile mother would join in. Soon she would send me to my room."

Over the next few weeks Cheryl was continued on suicide watch. But now she showed more curiosity, and she expended more energy in the unit's family life by helping with chores and by cooking and baking foods remembered from childhood Sunday dinners.

When she requested an end to suicide precautions and expressed a desire to explore the town alone, the staff deliberated for hours, debating the dangers of her pumped-up hypomanic emotion. They decided to monitor her condition hour by hour. As she improved, monitoring became day by day.

She followed the rules, always requesting passes, always home before dark. One night, unable to reach Lorna, she phoned me at the office to say she would be late.

At the next morning's session, Cheryl seemed alert but puzzled. "There must be something wrong with me," she said. "Each day I'm drawn to the Catholic church in town, the one with the graveyard. I sit alone in the back of the church until dark, and then I sit alone in the graveyard. I guess it's weird, but it makes me feel better. Sometimes I even feel good."

As Christmas approached, I found another note in my mailbox.

> The holidays are near and the north is cold. My folks are going to their winter home at Vero Beach. The ocean has always restored me. My niece and nephew will be there. If I love anybody, it's those two children. Please, may I go?

Was this a budding flower of life or was it a hoax, a resolution of certain death? Did she plan to walk out into the sea, or to take her mother's pills? Or both? Feigning assurance, I told her to make her plans.

On my desk the morning of her departure for the southern Gulf Coast of Florida, I found two long-stemmed roses, red and white, in a vase of water. A note read: "To my best friend. The red rose symbolizes love and the white rose means the opposite of death. I'm afraid to say the word (life)."

Not long after her arrival home, she sent me a letter in red ink saying that she was confused between her feelings of love and those of suicide. She fully had planned to kill herself on this trip, she said. She had not been sleeping, and she was frightened.

She was avoiding her father. She had witnessed her parents arguing. She had gone upstairs (with her Raggedy Ann doll), put a chair against the door, and contemplated slitting her wrists.

The letter continued:

> All day long, my mother keeps saying how hard she tried. My father had told her what you told him, that she kept me away from him. He keeps throwing that in my face. I was on the phone with a girlfriend, one of the few willing to talk to me, and he grabbed the phone. I felt violent, tried to call you, but you were out. I called the houseparents, but that didn't help. Now all parents sound as terrible as mine.
>
> My mood changes a thousand times a day. How can anybody with so many problems get well? I expect too much from you. I believe you can wave a magic wand over my head and make everything all right. When sitting in that cold graveyard, I decided to visit a minister. I felt convinced the devil had taken over my body. I killed Gail, and I'm doing the same to you and my parents. Wherever I walk, I turn the earth over. I found a notebook of Gail's here, and I see it was I who made her do it. I'm packing it to show you when I return.
>
> My sister made arrangements for me to receive electric shock treatments. I agreed and felt tremendous guilt. Today, my mother and I drove past some cliffs, and she wailed about wanting to

jump, but not having the guts to do it. I knew she blamed me. I feel so much guilt. The anxiety is driving me out of my skin. I would welcome depression. As I write, I feel my heart pounding in my throat, and my stomach is on fire. I feel loaded with speed, but have taken no drug. I eat day and night, trying to feel better. Even with this panic, I see blackness everywhere. I can't ever imagine finding peace, not for an hour, not for a minute, not for a second.

Sorry,
Cheryl

3. Misery Loves Company

Cheryl remained with her parents in Florida. Several days after her last letter, I received a phone call. In a weak and tremulous voice, she said she and her mother were sharing her mother's Valium, a fact unknown by the rest of the family. "Damn it, Cheryl," I shouted, "all our work is going down the drain! Get the hell back here as soon as possible."

It was four days before Cheryl arrived at the unit, but she was there, and she was alive. She immediately isolated herself in her bedroom, refusing dinner but announcing that she would keep her morning therapy session. I planned to use the session to distance her from any more attempts at suicide. It would be futile to try to extinguish thoughts of suicide; she would continue to have them anyway.

I explained that philosophers (such as Heidegger and Sartre) hoped to understand life by writing of its opposite, death. But nobody had ever returned from death. Metaphorically, Cheryl's serious attempt at the university, where Gail had succeeded, had also exceeded the boundaries of life. Had not her body been healthy enough to metabolize the toxins of the ingested medication and booze, she never would have awakened.

"You're way off, Doctor. You don't have the slightest idea of what's going on in my head."

"I know that you went to Florida, that you were

hopeful, feeling good before the trip. And that you sit here now, depressed, angry, and more suicidal than I have ever seen you."

"Go on, talk about the drugs now. Another lousy lecture." Pointing a finger, she said, "I swallowed my mother's medicine, three, four, seven, eight, probably ten at a time. I never asked for the pills. I don't care if you don't believe me. She pushed them on me."

"Where's all that love you felt when you left? The roses, the romantic notes."

"Give me some truth serum if you don't believe me, why don't you?"

"You've already doped yourself up on all that Valium. What's truth serum going to do for you?"

"Make me high. You shrinks, with your brain surgery, shock treatments, all of you are soul killers, life killers. *Killer, killer, killer.*" She was hammering her head against the chair's armrest. "Death is too beautiful for you to understand. You say death is your enemy. And I say you're just plain chicken."

I tolerated the vitriolic outburst, a form of negative transference. This is in contrast to the sweet and usually false niceness of positive transference portrayed in the media, advertising brochures, and cinema, where recovery from a nervous breakdown is typified by a smiling face. Any therapist who cannot take bombardments of insults and abusive hate, often voiced with the energy and force of a murderer, does not last long in the profession.

But how best to answer this bombardment?

"Sure, I'm afraid of death," I said. It wasn't my death I feared as much as hers—that seemed more imminent. "You're angry at me because I won't give you the truth serum."

I had a hunch that Cheryl, like most suicides, was really afraid of death. She wanted to kill not herself, but her misery. Those who succeeded had overwhelming anxiety, and believed they were going to die soon, anyway. Resigned to this belief, they wanted to control their fate. Even if my hunch was correct, I wasn't about to challenge her. This young woman could kill herself spitefully. She had left the security of The Clinic to go where there was easy access to drugs, as well as a big ocean, and she had returned alive. I was not going to confront her with some interpretation like "life has a hold on you," or my belief that she really did fear death. I did not want to give her reason to prove me wrong.

I said, "Life and death enter the world together. The moment someone is born, that person begins to die. Did you know that?"

She looked as if she were staring right through to the back of my head, so I continued. "Death is the only pure absolute. Life and death are contained within each other, they complement each other, and they are understandable in terms of each other. Hold back death, and we hold back life." I returned her stare. "More people kill themselves by taking drugs—sleeping pills and pain killers. So why do you, who like to be different, want to be ordinary?"

"You don't understand my pain."

"So what is your pain, beside your boring routine and habit?"

"I read that drugs are a substitute for love. It's probably bullshit, like everything else. Don't you dare think of getting close to me, you pervert. I hate men, and I wouldn't touch you with a ten-foot pole. I don't want any woman touching me, either."

"My hand is extended to you anytime you want it," I answered. "I'm sorry. I can join with you in your misery only so far."

"Then hold me. If you really want to make me feel better. I know it works. Gail and I would do downers, get numb, and hold each other and rock. That's something I never told anyone," she said sadly.

"Drugs and love don't mix."

Her sudden switch from anger to seduction left me doubting her real feelings. Perhaps she was beginning to trust me. If so, she might surrender some of her sickness. An agreement of barter: one drop of sickness for one drop of affection.

However, there was another side. She might close off her emotions, withdraw, and never again try. I had seen this happen in others. And would I be able to harness my own feeling? My need to cure her could be an Achilles heel.

Coquettishly, she begged, "Please hold me. Gail and

I always held each other when nothing else worked."

I felt panicky. I could say "Psychiatry is a talking therapy," or "You are still too immature, not a true woman," or simply, "No," and blame myself for being weak. These were all appropriate, safe answers, but what about the patient? We encounter obstacle after obstacle in the practice of psychiatry. Would this be as far as treatment could progress? If I threw myself into an emotional itinerary, offered her a bridge to life, would I end up consumed by the devil, with a loss of career, maybe even family?

I decided then and there to confer with an older and more experienced psychiatrist and analyst.

I held her hand, the one that she reached out toward me, and felt relieved. She hummed some unrecognizable but pleasant tune, then stopped.

"When I was a little girl and had a friend over, my mother would talk constantly, and my friend and I couldn't play alone. I guess my mother was jealous. I may have told you about that." She sucked her thumb as she spoke.

She said she had something to tell me that was embarrassing to her, and I encouraged her to talk about everything that came to her mind. She then described what she said was a strange and freakish feeling throughout her body. A flushing in the face, burning in the mouth, lips, and ears. The warmth traveled down her neck, into her chest, stomach, and crotch. The feelings were new to her and made her squirm, and she couldn't sit still. It was different and uncomfortable to feel this way, because she was accustomed to feeling dead.

"You're having a full battery of feelings, from infancy to adulthood, all at once," I responded. "When you felt nothing, it was less trouble, no anger, no eroticism, no anything. I believe you're discovering the path out of depression."

"I know more than you think I know," she said. "I didn't say anything for fear you would think me a bad person, but I've been putting my finger in my you-know-what the last few nights. I almost believe I had an orgasm, but I don't really know what that is."

The ringing of the phone ended this bizarre conversation, but not before I heard Cheryl say, "I wish we could spend the night together, just you and me alone." I didn't answer.

At eight the next morning, I sat opposite Dr. Adler in his office. "So, she wants to sleep with you," he said. "That's good. She enjoys your smell, your touch, and she wants to please you. You must be flattered. Do you really believe she loves you?"

"I don't know what to believe." Was Adler taunting me? Was he trying to get some message across to me? Even so, I felt safe in his analytic sanctum and I loosened up, letting my mind float.

Had I been too taken up by responsibility while I built up my practice at The Clinic? Did my absence from home and long hours with patients keep me from my own family? Was I foolish enough to see Cheryl as my repentance, my reparation for those long-ago errors?

"Do you want to go to bed with her?" Adler asked.

"Who, me?" The guy had uncanny insight. "No. Well, maybe, I'm not sure," I answered. He seemed unimpressed, and what was worse, offered no words of advice. In fact, he chose that moment to rise from his chair and leave the room. The session was over.

It was the evening rush hour and the city streets teemed with cars racing to the suburbs. I let my mind review the last hour. Why had I said "maybe"? I didn't really think that. I wasn't about to throw away everything because of this mission to cure, and just when I'd begun to feel some confidence in my work. But I needed help with this case.

February had come and gone, the residual snow turning gray as it melted. Crocuses broke ground even while March regaled us with fierce winds. With nature's awakening would come the anniversary of Gail's death. Cheryl reacted by withdrawing deeper, staying in her room, refusing to see anybody. Yet from this self-imposed entombment she kept a trickling of notes flowing to my mailbox. First, a barrage of hostility.

"You never cared. I saw Ann [another patient] kiss you at the conference. I hate you." Then, as if to exonerate me as a cause of her impending death, she poured out a river of sweet affection, assuring me she loved me yet hating to admit she needed me. She would remain in her room, enjoying the hermitage, her only distractions Coke after Coke, her cat, and a new antidepressant that she was asking to take.

As I walked to the car one evening, Lorna thrust a note into my hand and began to walk away. It read:

> Soon, when my life ends, I hope to be reborn into a more loving, happier family. If that should happen, I will be happy, but it will be in another life, not here. I need to sleep. It will not be like those other times I overdosed, not ill fated nor disheartening. It will be more exhilarating, even intoxicating.

I stopped Lorna with a shout. "Watch her every move!"

Nothing surfaced for a few days, but constant surveillance assured me Cheryl was alive.

Another communiqué followed. Written in black ink on a scrap torn from a brown bag, it read:

> I'll chance going to Hell—probably my final resting place. I'll try, but I don't think I have enough strength to leave this bed. The pain of living outweighs the pain of death. Joylessly, I realize the deep love I hold for you. I will miss that feeling. However, the forces of my dead friends have a magnetic pull. Sometimes when I think of you, Lorna, and The Clinic, an image of life becomes strong, but not strong enough. Yes, the happiest days of my life were here. Soon everybody will push me away, it is too close to continue. I could not take it, what with spring emerging. But you must not die. Too many depend on you for their survival. Don't consider yourself a failure. No doctor saves all his patients.

Her downward plunge continued, immune to all help. The treatment team debated whether to have Cheryl sleep in the lighted living room, where many eyes would view her, or to grant her wish to remain in the privacy of her room. It was decided she could remain in her room but a psychology student would remain in the hall just outside the door. One

morning, at the end of his shift, the student brought me
another note:

> I am no longer fighting to stay alive. I like nothing
> about life, and remain resigned to my fate. It is a
> matter of when now. I no longer find the strength to
> go to the kitchen where there are people. I no longer
> desire to face the houseparents. In the past, when
> faced with nothingness, memories of the ocean, the
> waves, the sand, the salt smell of the sea could bring
> me out of this. Pills, and cutting myself are all that
> remain. Oh, why did I come here? What do you see
> in life? To me, it is all one bad dream. This is my
> last note. Writing it all down only makes me worse.

At the bottom of the note was a bloody cross and written in
dry blood were the words, "I cannot live without drugs."

Working with people who space emotional crises
between short phases of relative quiescence is like living on
the edge of an active volcano. Long ago I learned to rest as
much as possible during the calm periods. This is no mean
feat, since I usually treat three or four active patients
concurrently. I have been tempted to medicate one or two of
these patients, letting them sleep via a chemical means,
thereby freeing my energy for one case at a time. But the
danger of medication permanently repressing awakening
emotions is real. As a result, I often feel like a fireman
rushing from one fire to another—with only one glass of
water in hand.

Reading Cheryl's bloody note, I felt as though a
cold steel rod had been jammed into my head, penetrated
my abdomen, moved downward to rest in the calves of my
legs. I had to come up with a new idea, another maneuver in
this war game between sickness and health.

The next morning my strength began to return as I
dressed. I called the unit, saying that I would be there in ten
minutes and asking them to gather the patients in the living
room for a general house meeting. Cheryl must be included,
and if she wouldn't leave her room, someone would have to
get her. She did come willingly. All eyes watched as she
stalked into the room, sullen, tight-mouthed, square-

shouldered. Her hair fell matted over her face, and she wore pajamas.

"I've got all your notes," I shouted, "and I refuse your wish to die!" Not even an echo answered.

She raised her head toward the heavens. Her hands were clenched. The next sound was a grating swish, and blood spurted like a pulsating fountain on the carpet.

Someone grabbed the razor. Blood fell everywhere. I applied a tourniquet even while she fought and kicked. "I'm going to die and no one will stop me!" she yelled.

We held her arms and assessed the damage. With suturing material and antiseptic, a nurse placed six stitches in Cheryl's left wrist and five in the right while Cheryl shouted, "You bastards! All of you! I'm leaving today. I'm getting a lawyer."

Every hospital has a Patients' Rights Committee, as mandated by the Department of Welfare regulations. The bill is inclusive, and one of its paramount provisions ensures that no patient will be held against his or her will without due process.

It seemed likely Cheryl would challenge her need for hospitalization and mount an argument defending her belief that she was not a danger to herself. However, her bandaged wrists bore witness to the contrary. The county magistrate, though often partial to the patient, was not foolhardy. If committed involuntarily (the law allows 21 days), a patient could choose to remain or transfer to the designated state institution.

Cheryl called the public defender and they conferred for about one and a half hours. The compassionate defender persuaded her to stay voluntarily, thus avoiding a court hearing and a sure involuntary commitment.

Returned to the unit, she was placed in a straightjacket and would sleep in a restraint sheet. Someone would stay by her side all night.

On my way home that evening, all manner of thought swept through my mind. If only she would let me inside her locked mind, that anagram of opposites: championship swimmer and thumb sucker, straight-A student yet naive about the simplest relationships. Once fiercely competitive, she now withdrew from everyday life. Once independent and self-disciplined, she now denied any need for human touch.

I felt sandwiched between opposing forces. It would be easy to transfer her to another hospital, to hope another doctor could do what I couldn't. However, I rarely gave up on a case if the family wanted me to continue.

4. Limbo

My request to see Dr. Adler was urgent, and he saw me as soon as he could. On the way to the city I gathered my thoughts, answering my own questions and rehearsing what I wanted to say. Did Cheryl want to leave, probably to go to another hospital? And if so, did I want her to go? Didn't I think she was already showing signs of being hooked on the treatment?

"So, Dr. Honig," Dr. Adler asked,"what do you think?"

"I don't know what to think. What are your ideas?"

There was a long pause before he said, "Do you know Dr. Randall, the head of the department at the university? He wrote that famous book on the magic of talk therapy. A classic in our field, right? He fucks most of his women patients, especially the pretty ones. Everybody knows it. I've had a few come to me and tell me of their experiences. Why has it remained a well-kept secret within the profession? They tell similar stories about other doctors, but it has never come out in public about Randall. Why? He keeps an elaborate diary with all his patients' birthdays, their children's names, and he writes to them."

That said, he left the room. On the return drive, I wondered why the hell Adler had told me that story. Dr. Randall, another icon with clay feet. So what, it wouldn't happen to me.

Cheryl had spoken about spending the whole night with me, but that was something I had faced with many patients before. Like many others, she made it sound as though her need was sexual. I believed it to be more basic: cuddling, holding, caring, simple fusion with another human. This was a universal phenomenon in the course of psychotherapy.

The next day, Cheryl met with her court-appointed attorney. In his opinion, she was a danger to herself and committable for twenty-one days under Pennsylvania law. If the judge agreed, she didn't have to stay at The Clinic but could go to the nearest state hospital. If she desired to remain at The Clinic voluntarily, there would be no need for a hearing. Faced with these choices, she agreed to stay.

She seemed relieved by the results of the hearing, which meant she didn't have to decide whether to stay or leave; the law had made that decision for her. She soon asked for another private session. When she came into my office and sat in the chair, she held a well-worn paperback book, the screenplay of *Face to Face,* a film by Ingmar Bergman. Had her enthrallment with Ann Sexton and Sylvia Plath been laid to rest? Had the relationship between Ingmar Bergman, the film director, and Liv Ullman, the Norwegian actress, the female lead in so many of his films, replaced that obsession? The name Liv, itself, meant life, love. Perhaps she had found a similarity between her own childhood and that of Ullman, in the symbiosis between mother and daughter, with the absence of a father.

I took the paperback in my hands and then returned it to her. "Would you like to hear some passages from my favorite movie?" she asked. "Sure, why not?" I answered. The book was a buffer, a way of diffusing, even devouring, intimacy. Despite all her fantasies of our being alone together, she was far from prepared for the actual moment.

Cheryl stood awkwardly, as if she were introducing a play. "Maria was the patient and Jenny, played by Liv Ullman, was the psychiatrist. Ready?"

> Have you never loved anybody, Jenny? (She laughs, stretching out her hand and lays it on Jenny's thigh). What would you say if I raised my hand and stroked your cheek? What would you say if I lowered my hand and began to fondle your breast?

> Jenny: You're sweet, really, and very persuasive. But you must remember that a psychiatrist often has to deal with this particular situation. The big problem, and it hasn't been solved yet, is how to avoid involvements between doctor and patient. I'm your doctor and I'm trying to make

you well. It's my responsibility how that's to be done.

> Maria: (Quietly) So you won't make love to me?

> Jenny: (With a smile) No, I certainly won't. But if you'd like to continue our inadequate attempts to make you well, I'll gladly do what I can.

Cheryl continued: "One of Jenny's patients asks her, 'Do you think someone can commit suicide out of a fear of death? It sounds crazy, but do you think it's possible?' Jenny says, 'It's not unusual.'"

In her autobiography, Liv Ullmann wrote of her experiences in therapy after her breakup with Bergmann. Her passages intimately discussed the involvement that takes place between a therapist and patient, especially the patient's feelings of love for the therapist. Whether that therapist is man or woman, the feelings are the same, and are most often expressed in sexual language. (These feelings are especially confusing when the therapist is of the same sex as the patient.)

Cheryl stopped reading and said, "I, too, have a horrendous fear of death. That's a confession, Al."

She placed the book on the desk. "I've been thinking about many things. I was too involved with my own suffering and terror to help Gail. We latched on to each other in a crazy way. We seemed to be two victims from the devastation of a war. She was a timid person paralyzed by internal dread, and she felt a lot of disillusionment and sorrow mixed with anger.

"Al, the night before I went to my room to take all the pills, I bought a giant jelly donut, my favorite food, for my last meal. At twelve noon, I returned to the room, removed my jeans, swallowed all the pills, and placed a sign on the door stating I had gone home for the weekend and would return Monday. Then I locked the door, fell on the bed, curled up, and closed my eyes.

"Gail, in the other bed, took two bottles of a heavy tranquilizer and downed them with a half bottle of rum. We weren't lovers, but a strong bond existed between us."

She stood up and began to pace, alternating between

thumping her chest and wringing her hands."She's left me here alone. I'm like a child in the dark determined not to call out because no one will answer. Guilt is eating out my insides. Why, why, why?" She raised her head and stared at the wall."Gail never used street drugs, never drank. And she always took medicine as prescribed. I turned her on to abusing drugs."

Her eyes became misty. "I remember one spring when I was in my own apartment. I was eighteen, and a helpless little girl. I felt only constant terror, and whenever it became unbearable, I'd swallow handfuls of pills and get my stomach pumped. I didn't care anymore, told nobody. Eight times I overdosed, leaving the outcome to fate.

"One weekend I asked my mother for a Valium. She handed me a whole bottle. Was it a mistake or deliberate? I went back to my apartment and took everything. She must have realized what she'd done because she came to the apartment, and I found myself in the emergency room again. I limped back to college that fall. Soon after that, it all happened."

She squeezed my hand. "I would love for you to hold me tight, but I won't ask you to get involved any more than you are comfortable in doing."

I smelled her fetid breath and wondered why every patient with a mental illness let their teeth rot. That, and the stale odor of sweat and unwashed clothing, acted as a safeguard against intimacy.

"I've lost the fear of dying," she said, "of ending up in Hell, but I can't understand the fear I have of drugs. Drugs have saved me from death more than once. My pet name was 'Overdoselettes.' My emotions were killed for a while, believe me. My father objected violently to my drug use, and I hated him for it. Obviously, I identified with my mother."

She turned her back to me, withdrawing into an icy freeze, a pattern all too familiar. Her actions were predictable up to a point: first affection, then willful violence meant to destroy. This duality was exemplified by the African violet that appeared on my desk one day, with a note of love—only to be uprooted and torn to shreds the next. Or the telltale blood on the window frame through which she'd punched her hand. Or the pillow she'd made with the teddy bear stitched so tenderly, then ripped to shreds after I told her father of the gift when he phoned.

These undulating mood swings were tempered by long silences. The awkward quiet might be broken by, "I do love you, but not enough to want to live. Every moment is filled with raw pain. You keep me from suicide, temporarily. I have contacts with a woman doctor in Philadelphia. She will sell me any drug I want, but I'm too exhausted to go. When I stop taking drugs, I overeat sweets. I'm ballooning up again. Look at me."

"I don't think you look so bad," I said. "Just start to exercise again."

"I'm split. One part of me wants to join all those people who killed themselves. Another part says Hell and Satan are all around, and Satan will force me to kill myself. I'm weak. I need my mother and I need the ocean. I don't deserve your love, and I fear you will leave me before it's all over."

"You'll be doing the leaving first, probably for a younger person, and that's fine with me," I replied.

"Please don't say that, it's hurting my ears. What's the use, I need my mother, I need my drugs, and I'm going to die, anyway."

Cheryl faced me. I tried to ignore her stale breath and the smell of her unwashed clothes as my mind began to wander.

What would be my role in this case? My fantasy was to become the "mother of life," to create a primitive bond, an imprint through a transfer of emotion from doctor to patient. With patients such as Cheryl, this was difficult to achieve with classical psychoanalytic therapy but easier with the involvement of all five senses and the mama mumbo of "mother talk," the slow, rhythmic, positive feeding language that one might use when reading a youngster a story.

She must have felt that I disapproved of her appearance, for she said, "I can't believe you can even like me. I'm not pretty, not intelligent, not even strong. Yet I feel that you do. Maybe that's what trust is, I don't know. I don't think either you or Lorna would harm me. Both of you understand and it's easy talking to you. I often wonder what you might be to me. Mother? Strangely, I see you as a baby, especially when you are tired. Then I want to feed you a bottle and hold you in my arms. I want to help you when there are difficulties around The Clinic.

"Other times, I imagine us as lovers, like Liv and Ingmar. Please listen, I want to read some passages from *Changing,* Liv Ullman's autobiography." In this book, Ullman wrote of the contrast between her public life and her yearning for love. She wrote of the joys and mistakes she made in her five-year relationship with Ingmar Bergman, a relationship that gave birth to her daughter, Linnet. Cheryl, step by step in her recovery, was identifying with Liv Ullman.

She flipped the well-worn , stained, and wrinkled pages and read:.

> Nights when we lay close to each other and he whispered that I must be quiet so that he, in the stillness, could long for me and ask me to talk to him again. Our boundless need for each other, for what the other one should represent. The powerlessness when something went wrong. I sought the absolute security, protection—a great need to belong.

"Dr. Honig, I have a letter I want to show you. I wrote it to my mother when I was seven."

She groped through a stack of papers and found a penciled stick-figure drawing of a little girl with hands outstretched, wearing a print dress, with a flower at its side. She read:

> Dear Mommy, I'm very sorry I've been mean to you. How are you feeling? I hope you are feeling better. Is there anything I could get you or do? I will be glad to do it. I love you very much. I hope you will get much better than you have ever felt. Are you feeling better? Tell me and if you aren't, I will come and get you away if you want me to. Are you having a good time? If you aren't, I will read to you and play a game or let you go to sleep. I love you very much. Love, Cheryl

"Mother was in the mental hospital," she explained. "It shows that I've changed very little in all these years."

Cheryl was not yet out of danger. True, there were beginning signs of positive attachment, but the suicide thoughts lingered. Now, I believed, was the time to distance her from death.

I said, "Camus, Modigliani, Virginia Wolfe, Hemingway were all recognized geniuses, and all were suicides. Wasn't it Camus who said that an act like this is prepared within the silences of the heart as in the great work of art? Pathetic! Every one of them is a tragedy. Disconnected people who caved in!"

Why was I saying this? Who was I reassuring? Was all this one-sided opposition, my pushing and pulling to keep her alive, getting to me?

"Some say a suicide is like an exorcism," I blurted, "an attempt to kill that rotten part we hate within ourselves. If we cut it out, we can emerge reborn. Oh, wasn't it wonderful that in some stage of evolution, man discovered that he could kill not only other animals and his fellow man, but also himself. It can be assumed that life has never been the same to him since."

Cheryl climbed out of her chair and began to shout. "Some more of that shrink stuff, huh, Doctor? All you shrinks are alike. And all this hand holding. I bet you five it's an act to get me well. Some psychiatric technique so you can write a paper, hoping it will make you famous. All of you are callous, depraved, unfeeling!"

Shaken, I stiffened up abruptly. We were shouting at each other. "What the hell are you pissed about now?" I asked, my voice hoarse and heavy. Her accusations inflicted pain, and she knew it. Was she testing my ingenuousness? Or was she flogging the psychiatric profession *tout ensemble,* or the many healers who were never able to help either her or her mother?

All of a sudden her voice became calmer.

"As we are back to the topic of suicide, Doctor, I want to make a statement. Once a person decides on suicide, everything anybody says or doesn't say, someone not saying good morning, an angry glance, a wrong telephone call, a person talking too much about him or herself—all are taken as rejections. Everything hurts too damn much. Why was I the chosen one? My sisters escaped the devastation. And my mother objected to my writing anyone. She was always angry when I used the telephone. You read that letter I wrote to her when I was seven. I have another letter where I say I want to marry her, my own mother." She paused. "Suppose I told you that I was in love with you. What would you do?"

I withdrew my chair to a narrow corner of the room, hoping that changing positions might help me think more clearly. I had been working steadily overtime for the last several days. With lowered resistance, my barriers were down. And Cheryl knew it. It was as if our vulnerabilities had danced together in some strange ballet, and with this duet she was moving further and further away from the illness.

I felt ecstatic, as one feels when sharing intimacy with another human being. Cheryl, in spirit, was inside me. I reflected upon similar feelings in the past, remembering the analyst to whom I would bring presents, and with whom I wanted to be with every moment, and with whom I believed myself in love: a man. So I understood Cheryl.

"What makes you think you are in love with me?" I had regained some therapeutic composure.

"I want to be with you all the time, to hold your hand, to gaze into your brown eyes. I would do anything you ask. I realize you won't be able to love me as much as I love you. I'm scared, and I'm seeing that this is all too much for me, and could be my undoing. Perhaps I am hurting you, but you've taught me not to lie. I have lied and fooled many people. No one understood my despair because I hid my misery with a cheerful face."

Her tone had become dauntless. "Al, I want to make love, take my clothes off, hold you and make love, now."

I became paralyzed internally. Sure, she could throw away her clothes and all propriety. She had little to lose, and could finish having made a conquest. She was surrendering her sickness, but she was making me the substitute. She had begun to imitate my facial idiosyncrasies, patterns of speech. When she walked, it was with my gait. It was as if she were my clone.

But I imitated her. Her humor, her southwestern accent, her reckless ness. I heard Jenny's soul-shivering words, "The big problem...is how to avoid involvements between doctor and patient," but, in my conviction that without some sort of involvement there would be no cure, I only half believed them. Still, the responsibility was awesome, and I was unsure how it would end.

Even though Cheryl spoke boldly of lovemaking, was she able to sustain a relationship? She barely managed each day, and when she did, it was with interminable inner struggle. My job now was to be her teacher, to point out her weaknesses, and to challenge them.

But I could not deny that our shared emotion had ever happened. To do so would mean I had tricked her and lied to her. If I did that, I knew she would never trust me or perhaps anyone else again. I could say nothing that might shame her feelings, nor could I deny mine; if the doctor is too cowardly to acknowledge his or her own emotion, it is hypocrisy to encourage the patient to do so. Yet to give in to her wish would abort her therapy, for it would make all too human the illusion, and deny her dreams. So I must say no to an affair, but yes to the expression of love.

"Oh, how wonderfully reckless it would be to give in to our passions. But, sadly, there is tomorrow to face the world again."

"I understand," she replied quickly, with what sounded like relief.

"Whom do you love more, me or your mother?" I asked.

She paused, her lips pursed, coughed into a hankerchief she was holding tightly, and then responded.

"That's a hard question and I'd rather not answer it. But I've got to do something. Maybe, if I try, and I am unable to live for myself, I can live for you. Every time my mother says she's dying, I die too. And she always lies. I picked up the habit. But let's face it, my baby needs are greater than my sexual needs."

I must keep trying, I thought.

5. Fruit Tarts, Brownies, and Babies

Cheryl remained an inpatient, venting her creative urge by baking fruit tarts and pies, cakes and brownies—all a measure of her increasing emotional strength and self-esteem. Her sessions were filled with life force and happy daily occurrences. With optimism, she volunteered to work with a physician hospitalized at The Clinic after a suicide attempt. Lonely and despondent after a divorce and a forced separation from two small children, he became energized and intrigued by Cheryl's daily visits.

Hearing of her new activities, Big Jim refused to pay for further inpatient care. A fragile and somewhat embittered Cheryl moved reluctantly to the transition house in the next town where residents were charged with individual responsibility, very unlike the cushioning security at The Clinic.

Despite her insecurities, she made the transition fairly well and continued her volunteer work with her patient. But she refused further treatment, saying either she couldn't afford it or "talking never really helped."

As she struggled with a fluctuating self-image, I struggled with a diagnosis. No longer was the depression constant, nor was she obsessed with death; yet these symptoms came and went, as did her moods.

She retained contact by almost daily phone calls, usually during dinner (somewhat upsetting to my wife and family who cherished this precious time together). I took up my role as listener, a leader in good cheer, and her phone calls usually ended in a pep talk attempting to nullify the misery.

Most of the calls were disarmingly desperate, disclaiming any reason to stay alive. Yet little of this showed in her daily activity. Getting through each day was a victory in itself, not unusual for those attempting a transition from dependence to independence.

However, she was noticeably inexperienced in daily living, unable to make the tough, matter-of-fact, continuous decisions that enable people to engineer each day. Always fighting boredom, she refused to enter after-care groups. She also refused the factorylike assembly line of the sheltered workshop. Her impulsive outbursts had the ferocity of exploding scud missiles. Her room was in shambles and she had laid waste to her possessions, but she no longer cut her arms, and she enjoyed baby-sitting some of the younger staff's children.

Remaining in the area, she volunteered to house-sit and watch our dogs when my wife and I went on vacation or attended conferences. She went on to complete a B.A. at Rider College and an M.A. at the Wharton School in Business Administration. She was hired as a junior investment officer in a large suburban firm.

She ventured into one-at-a-time relationships with men. With little experience in the give and take of such relationships, she invested her all and demanded nothing—much as she had done with her mother. In these relation ships she was obedient, as she was with her father. She emerged selfless and faceless after the usual abandonment, wondering what went wrong.

She befriended married couples and baby-sat their children, sometimes becoming emotionally involved with the husband. Predictably, the wife would find out and the relationship would end with acrimony. Guilt, bulimic anorexia, and suicidal depression always followed. But, after much despair, as a substitute, she discovered jogging and accompanied a group on the 22-mile marathon-training run every Sunday.

When Big Jim's health began to fail, he became preoccupied with his impending death. Cheryl's visits to Texas were full of gloom as his health continued to worsen.

After his death and funeral, Cheryl requested a session, her first in several years. She had had a frightening dream: her father was alive, and he chased her with a butcher's knife. Cheryl felt panic, combined with a fear that the whole world was coming to an end. This was followed by a compulsion to preempt that destruction by cutting her throat. The compulsion lessened after the therapy session, and she did no cutting.

Soon afterwards, she became involved with the branch manager at her investment office. "I have no life without him," she cried, as she sat in the consulting chair opposite me, her face pallid and fearful, shoulders slumped, hands limp in her lap.

"He called yesterday, saying he never lied to me, but

that itself was a lie. He was renting a room to a girl who was seeing one of the guys at the office. This girl is a phony and I hate her. Nobody likes her. She is a Satan. She wants him, he's so seductive with women."

She wondered why women settle for so little. "And he's angry because I'm telling my friends about our affair. He wants to control me in every way, just like my father. He's hiding behind his wife, acting as if it never happened.

"Well, I sent her [his wife] a letter," she said, "describing the whole affair. It's been going on almost eight months. My landlord has seen him coming into my apartment, so I have a witness. He's telling people at the office that I'm crazy....

"Friends tell me he puts women down. He's mean. I'll never trust men again. And I'll never give so freely of myself again. And I can't keep getting involved like this. What is really so great about being alive, anyway? I guess this guy was a mother to me. But my pushy sisters contributed to my illness, too. They only cared about themselves, never considered me."

She had imagined she and her lover would be together forever. "He pursued the affair, and I adored him....But he says he never made any promises to me. Most everybody thinks I'm upset because my father died.

"You know, the only real mother I had as a child was Anna Mae, the colored maid. She loved me a lot but drank just as much. She worked every day, even Sunday. And Sunday is my worst day for depression."

Cheryl went on to stalk this man and his wife, confronting them in a restaurant parking lot near their home. She continued to write to the wife, telling her the affair wasn't her imagination.

She believed the branch manager was accumulating evidence against her, some real, some fictitious, in an attempt to dismiss her from the firm. I advised her to meet with a lawyer. The lawyer wrote a strong letter to the man, telling him there was ample evidence to prove the affair was real, and that it was sexual harassment if he attempted to fire his client.

Cheryl finally realized that pursuing this relationship was wasted energy, and that she wasn't really in love with him. She asked for a session and admitted to a dogged stubbornness, which she believed was mostly fueled by her inability to face her father's death.

After another eight months, she called and asked for another session. It was then that I noticed her puffy face, her heavy-lidded eyes, her swollen fingers. The diamond engagement ring she wore was tight on her third finger, left hand.

"I'm very uncomfortable. My breasts are enlarged. I've missed two periods. The pregnancy test is positive. With everything that has happened to me in the past, I never believed that I could conceive, so we didn't bother about birth control.

"Toni is Israeli; you know I always liked Jewish men. He works with me at Merrill Lynch."

Her young man was divorced, with two young children, whom Cheryl had met and liked. They had planned a big summer wedding in Austin, but her mother and sisters were suspicious at first. They believed the young man was after her money. "But he won them over—especially Mom," she said.

With the news of her pregnancy, they decided to marry at the Episcopal church in town. "Can you and your wife be there?" she asked.

The wedding was simple and joyous. Her mother attended, accompanied by a niece and a nephew; soon after that, the family was reconciled. Her last months of pregnancy were uneventful and she carried to term, delivering a healthy seven-pound girl.

I continue to hear from Cheryl, mostly by telephone. Toni has transferred to Merrill Lynch's office in New York, where they now live. Cheryl stayed at home after the birth of her daughter, planning to return in one year to her job with the brokerage firm. But when the time came, she and Toni decided she would remain home for another year, because "the baby needs me more than we need the money."

After the second year, she phoned saying she planned to visit. "You and your wife are like grandparents to our growing family," she said. She was pregnant again. Soon she was busy with another infant, a boy.

"I want to visit you and The Clinic, but I'm sure I

won't know anyone there. I guess it's different now, with managed care. I was fortunate to be there when time and money weren't the primary determinants as they are today."

When the deadline for her return to work approached, she and Toni once more thought it best that she remain a full-time stay-at-home mother, feeling this would pay the biggest dividends later. "It will be this way until the children are old enough for school, and then we'll see," she said.

Chapter III
A Modern Joan

1. A Medical Merry-Go-Round

> The character of Joan of Arc is unique. It can be
> measured by the standards of all time without
> misgiving or apprehension as to the result. Judged
> by any of them, judged by all of them, it is still
> flawless, still ideal, still perfect; it still occupies the
> loftiest place possible to human attainment, a loftier
> one than has been reached by any other mere
> mortal.

Compte, *Joan
of Arc*

Joan Cadwallader was three weeks shy of her eighteenth
birthday when she sought treatment at The Clinic. She sat
across from me, flanked by her family: her father, Herbert, a
physicist at a major university, tall, bent over, and ungainly,
a physicist associated with a major university; her mother,
Margo, solemnly attractive and stylishly dressed; and her
sister, fifteen-year-old Sarah. All sat quietly, cautiously
erect, not knowing what to expect.

"Why are you here?" I asked Joan. This was a
routine question designed to break through the leaden
hostility and help me determine how much a patient
understands about what is happening to herself and to her
world.

"I'm getting shock treatments," she answered. "I
had my forty-first yesterday. I don't mind, they don't hurt.
In three or four days I can remember almost everything
again. But the doctors are scared to continue."

Her family sat there, all of one expression: angry to have to repeat their story to yet another doctor, frightened that their whole lives would be placed in turmoil again. And for what? They no longer expected anything to improve.

"Look at my family," Joan said, pointing in turn to each one of them. "No one seems to know what else to do."

"About what?" I asked.

She spoke haltingly, with a fading angelic pallor which portrayed an obvious need for fluids. With skin the turgor of dried bark, and weighing less than 100 pounds, she belonged more to heaven than to earth.

"They say I have a compulsive disorder. I think in numbers, and my mind works at six different levels. My compulsive list is awesome, at least the size of three Bibles. And it's getting worse. I've been opening car doors, reaching out to touch the road as I drive along. So far, I haven't jumped out. I've been rushing into walls," she said, pointing to a reddened scar on her forehead.

"What will you do if the impulses become too strong?"

"I've told my mom. No one else has to know." A horrifying silence followed her words. There could be little doubt that suicide had been discussed.

"I remember back when I was three," she said as if she had memorized a report in Latin. "I had to step on cracks, burrs, and prickly chestnuts, and I had to touch flies. Then, later, the kids at school were mean. They cursed at me, made fun of the way I ate. I quit school, you know."

After a pause, she went on. "I've had every medication there is, and nothing helps." An inappropriate half grin settled on her parched lips.

At this first interview, her father said that insanity and suicide ran in his family, and alcohol abuse in his wife's family. He also mentioned that Joan's mother stayed home until Joan was four years old, then went back to school to obtain a degree in accounting. She later found a job with a tax firm.

Margo added, "I always thought there were too many baby sitters. The first one told wild stories that terrified Joan, the second one was overly religious, and the third one insisted that the children be constantly good." As

I listened to her, it occurred to me that this woman harbored many secrets.

The parents expressed a desire to talk without the children present. The Clinic's resident dogs, Ace and Myo, were with us, so Professor Cadwallader asked the girls to take them into the next room. Later, these dogs would sit in on every session with Joan.

Alone with his wife and me, Dr. Cadwallader confessed to a seventeen-year love affair with another woman. "I told Joan all about it as soon as she was old enough to understand," he said, but he was unable to tell his younger daughter. Mrs. Cadwallader said she didn't care if his relationship continued.

Both parents wanted Joan admitted to The Clinic immediately, with the proviso that she be driven back to the previous hospital to complete the course of electric shock treatments, since Dr. Cadwallader had noticed "mild improvement" during the past week. He wasn't sure whether this improvement was due to the combination of medications—a pill to control emotional outbursts, an antidepressant, and a tranquilizer—or to the electric shock. Both parents were skeptical of any form of psychotherapy, with Dr. Cadwallader saying it never had any effect on Joan's condition.

I suggested that the shock treatment be stopped immediately, as it was obvious from the examination that Joan was suffering from some memory loss and I wasn't sure why. However, this was academic because I was committed to my present caseload for at least four or five more months. Joan returned to the other hospital. In the interim, there were many calls from her parents inquiring when a bed would be available.

Four and a half months later, the professor and his family were back at The Clinic because, as he put it, "you are the only psychiatrist Joan has ever talked with, and you and she have similar tastes in books" (as if this latter point were important to her treatment!). Joan sat crossing herself frantically, saying she didn't want her parents to die.

"I don't blame you," I said. "It must work because they're both alive. And if you don't do it, and something happens, you'll never forgive yourself."

Soon she was on the floor with Ace and Myo. Ace was a bear-sized, arthritic golden retriever with dark, reddened eyes and a soft, cold black nose. Myo was a runty sad-faced St. Bernard with fluffy ears and a phlegmatism that could hypnotize soap. Together, they worked the halls and rooms of mental wards, defusing violence.

When anger fused red and white, Ace would turn on his back and roar like a lion, while Myo would emit loud moans and yowls to the moon. In a room heavy with the leaden cargo of depression, either dog would offer a paw to the sufferer and persist until all misery was driven away and the dog was petted in appreciation.

Joan, stroking both dogs, said that she was back "only to see them again." She added, "I'll come here only if you promise to treat me without drugs."

"You're very brave," I replied.

On her mental status exam she had not been able to remember where she was or the approximate time. ("Is today Tuesday? I don't remember much.") She seemed to be alarmed, and she held her head with both hands.

"You'll remember everything again in a week or two," I said, trying to reassure her.

It was difficult to ascertain the distinction between what was her short-term memory loss due to electric convulsive therapy and what was her inability to comprehend what was happening to her. She denied having hallucinations or delusions, or that she would ever become "insane." She admitted to putting her parents on a pedestal, believing she must protect them.

After her admittance, the family carried her one suitcase and sundry paraphernalia to the unit with funereal precision. Joan toddled behind them, jumping wildly in the air, bunny-hopping and leaping with feet approximated and knees stretched to her chest.

When her parents and sister left for home, she curled into a fetal position in a corner of the living room couch, a small brown teddy bear pressed against her abdomen, completely debilitated, looking like a street dweller from the Warsaw ghetto. Long, bony fingers moved like windup toys to an unrecognizable rhythm. She spent the night alone, refusing food and drink and never wanting to use the bathroom.

She awoke before daylight and carefully staked out her territory, like a muskrat or raccoon, by marking the corner of the couch with a flood of her own urine. There she sat, rigid, with closed eyes. But not for long. She suddenly began flailing her arms like a windmill, so rapidly that neither the raw eye nor a camera could have captured a pure image. The room rocked from her movements and reverberated with echoes of "Love, love, love, Sarah."

Then she passed so close to the plate-glass window that three staff persons had to bring her to the floor and secure her with a straightjacket and ankle cuffs. Once safe, she began a soft, undecipherable muttering with the rapidity of a typewriter: "Love, Mommy, Joan is a good girl. Me, Sarah, me, Daddy, me, Mommy." All this was uttered in the monotone chant of a Hari Krishna.

Unit activity began each morning at seven. Patients awake, toilet, shower—all spurred on by the cheers of one another and the sizzling sounds of bacon and eggs frying in the kitchen.

Joan, still bundled like an Apache baby in swaddling cloth, watched and absorbed the scene. Several hours later, somewhat subdued, her urine and feces permeating the living room, she was released from the restraints and was carried into the whirlpool bath. This ritual would be repeated every morning. At breakfast, still refusing food and fluids, she would stare at the fingers of her right hand and scream, "Life, me, Sarah, me, Mommy, kill, kill."

Late one afternoon not long after Joan had been admitted (time raced as fast as she did—I thought she had been there much longer), her father visited her before leaving to attend an academic conference. With shouts of "Daddy, Daddy, Sarah, Sarah," she looked at him with adoring eyes while drinking six ounces of apple juice he had brought her. (Thank you, God, for small things, I thought.)

The morning trips from the living room couch where she was sleeping nightly (for extra protection) to the bathroom whirlpool became a regular daily stint. Routine such as this provided basic structure and warmth that, through repetition of time, place, and person, became as comforting to her chaotic psyche as it might be to a newborn.

Joan loved to play in the tub with her feces, like a baby with a toy boat. Then, dried, powdered, and diapered, she was dressed in a hospital gown and slippers. The living room had become her bedroom. New furniture was added for everyone's comfort along with a rocking bed (an old hospital bed with rounded welded cradles) and a feeding chair used by geriatric patients. She was considered the neediest person in the unit, and was surprisingly accepted by the other patients who had experienced similar regression on their journey toward growth and eventual recovery.

Equally surprising, Joan would rise from the chair and walk down the hallway to answer her mother's daily phone calls. Who could have predicted that in this debilitated condition, she would have an animated conversation for some fifteen minutes? After the phone call she always returned to a nearly lifeless puppetlike position.

Joan continued to take nourishment, but usually only when her father visited—a glass of juice, some water. When he stayed for supper, she would eat ground meat, mashed potatoes, corn on the cob. After his departure she always suffered greatly (was it because he had visited or because he had left?). In the midst of shrieks that rocked the walls, she would fling herself from the chair to the floor, and thump her right hand with enough force to crack more than one bone.

When she was tied, for safety's sake, in the geriatric chair, she would lift it from its moorings. Her thighs and calves were blackened. She would pound her ears as though tortured by voices. She tried to blind herself, poking her fingers into her eyes until posy gloves (large canvas mittens) had to be placed on her hands.

All her prior medications had been tapered off, so she was basically drugfree, but at her obvious intense distress I ordered an injection of thorazine. I had not forgotten my promise to treat her without drugs, but it seemed cruel not to offer some relief. I rationalized that the medicine was prescribed only when required, and not as a steady diet. But would the decision to give her this merciful injection come back to haunt me? Had I given her a reason to say I had violated the trust that was so salient to a therapeutic relationship?

Most of the time Joan remained still as wood, with her hands hanging limply. Usually she kept her eyes closed; when she did open them, she focused on a maple tree outside the living room window.

She ambulated with the help of a wheelchair. This made it easier for her to go from living room bed to bathroom, and also to join the family for meals.

She finally emerged from her catatonia. She would chew and mouth her food like a tortoise and then spit everything on the floor. She was fond of chocolate pudding, and she caked her face with it as though it were mud. She acknowledged no acquaintance with table etiquette (apparently manners had never been important at home; evidently the family signaled the end of a meal by throwing food around the room and at one another, rocking, and shouting "love, love, love"). She later revealed that if she didn't shriek these words, her sister Sarah would burn in eternal Hell. The whole scenario was not unlike some strange personal orthodox faith.

Pray, what might be the prognosis for this unfortunate young woman?

In recent years, more effort has been made to bring psychiatry into the mainstream of medicine. Most everyone, professional and layman alike, seems convinced that a genetic and biochemical origin exists in these baffling illnesses of the mind. We no longer talk of mental illness but, instead, of brain disorder and severe brain disease.

The interesting debates—whether mental illness is myth, and whether psychiatrists are really treating personal, social, and ethical problems in living—no longer take place.

Joan Cadwallader, during her many hospital stays, had been diagnosed variously with schizophrenia, schizoid personality disorder, narcissistic personality disorder, and, most often, obsessive compulsive disorder. Perhaps the most telling reports came from the National Institutes of Mental Health (NIMH) where Joan, at age fourteen, was intensively studied as part of a research project that looked into Obsessive Compulsive Disorder (OCD).

"Joan Cadwallader," declared the researchers at NIMH, "fits into that four percent of our study that had more than the run of the mill OCD. We are still struggling to find a diagnosis for her."

I, too, was becoming obsessed. In many ways, our obsessions were somewhat alike. Joan's rituals were a set of chess plays designed to save her family from death and extinction. And as I observed this extravaganza, was I not shaping a set of ideas and actions of my own, a stratagem to save my patient's life? My belief in a plan was every bit as beset as was hers. Thus it became even more difficult to arrive at a definitive diagnosis. Perhaps I could bask in the smugness of brotherhood with my colleagues at clinical case discussions, seeing her as a very unusual case of Obsessive Compulsive Disorder. Nevertheless, to apply the statistical manual, I would have to shift gears and employ coolness and some distance, even some degree of removal. I wasn't sure it would work as a therapeutic tool because it had already been applied to Joan many, many times, and always without success.

Unlike the compulsions of eating, sex, or gambling, Joan's obsessions and compulsions gave no pleasure. Nor did they grant her any power to control her world, even when she performed her rituals "just right." I asked myself whether she, in enacting her rituals, was any different from any of us who must master the repetitions of daily life—work, marriage, ongoing relationships with relatives and friends—the successful repetition of which leads to ordinary pleasure and a happy life. When I felt her suffering, I concluded that I wouldn't want anyone to go through what every day and every night was for Joan.

I was completely puzzled by Joan's rapid explosions of emotion that felt like the firing of gasoline in a combustion engine. These explosions were followed by periods of paralysis. Had she been sexually abused? She had been heard screaming, "No! No! Don't. No more. Stop. Oh, God, oh, Lord." Was she reliving a sexual attack?

Up to that point, my role had been that of a scene supervisor, a director. To play a lead in this drama would require round-the-clock participation. This I had done before. In training, I had slept next to a huge violent catatonic who, trusting no one, had frightened everyone away. Every morning upon awakening, I had removed the ammonia- and feces-soaked restraints and placed him in a warm tub. I then powdered and baby-oiled his skin, dressed him, and took him out into the world for whatever he could do that day. After nine months (curiously, catatonia often lasts about as long as gestation), he emerged from catatonia, and we rode to the Psychiatric Institute in Philadelphia to show the unfolding miracle. But it was not to last. One day he said, "Al, everything is black. It's too much." He spent his remaining days in a state institution. I collapsed in exhaustion.

Was Joan to meet the same fate? The treatment had reached a plateau. She consumed the houseparents, the family assistants, and all the patients in the cottage. She took everything, gave nothing, and still would not speak to anyone around her.

I would have to train someone to work with her in the role of a neomother, much as a coach prepares a runner for the Olympics, in subtle movements of rhythm and flow: when to approach, when to lay back, how long to stay. And when inertia occurred I would have to transfuse my emotion into the situation.

I did not have long to wait. Her one-sided pattern of take and more take had now become compulsion number one for me.

I decided that a shocking directive might arouse enough emotion to reconnect the flow of energy. "You are such a mess!" I shouted at her. "Your whole family wants to get rid of you!"

Upon hearing these words, meek Joan awoke from her lethargy and erupted from the couch like a dasher from the starting blocks, arms cocked like two lances. I felt one of her fingers in each eye. Temporarily blinded and seeing stars, I heard racing feet, then the crash of the plate-glass window as it shattered from the impact of Joan's forehead. Blood and screams echoed through the unit.

When Joan was examined, it was determined that no arteries or large veins had been punctured. She was as experienced in bashing against glass as a football lineman in hitting a tacking dummy head on. After the wounds were dressed, a motorcycle helmet was placed on her head and posy gloves covered both hands.

She has had an easy laugh, but
it was gone now; she had been
born for comradeship, and
blithe and busy work, and all
manner of joyous activities.
But here was only dreariness,
leaden hours, weary inaction,
brooding stillness, thoughts
that traveled day and night,
round and round in the same
circle, and wear the brain and
break the heart with
weariness. It was death in
life, yes, death in life, that
is what it must have been.
And there was another hard
thing about it all. A young
girl in trouble needs the
soothing solace and support
and gentle ministries which
only these can furnish; yet,
in all these months of gloomy
captivity in her dungeon, Joan
never saw the face of a girl
or woman. Think how her heart
would have leaped to see such
a face.

Compte, *Joan
of Arc*

Sandra Williams, a chubby middle-aged mother of two
teenagers, drifted into the vacuum. She became Joan's
rescuer. It was she who began the portage of this
undernourished and parched body from restraint bed to
bathtub. She brought in toy boats to float along with the
feces. When Joan flailed like a spinning top, Sandra
consoled her with warm compresses to her head. When
Joan sobbed in pain, Sandra held and rocked her.

In reviewing this case, I discovered a clinical infant
study relevant enough to excerpt.

A mother and son illustrated the inherent difficulties in establishing regulatory and attachment mechanisms with a newborn. Mother suffered from her own chaotic childhood, marked by psychological rejection and abandonment that terminated in a mental breakdown. Overt ambivalence toward both her pregnancy and her son's birth followed. She became depressed with her inability to nurture her child.

The child became easily irritable and was not readily consoled. He had tense musculature and many tremors and startles. He showed poor orientation to face and voice, and gaze aversion was noticed as early as the first month.

Given mother's suspicions and already intense ambivalence, we feared she would interpret her baby's behavior as a rejection of her as a mother, setting up a dangerous cycle in which the mother's pain and anger lead to rejection and withdrawal from the child.

The child had difficulty orienting to his environment. Although cuddly, his own attempts at self-quieting (taking his hand to his mouth) were unsuccessful. A month later, the condition deteriorated. Obviously, his environment was not helping him.

Such deterioration in an infant's capacity for regulation and interest in the world is an extremely worrisome sign. There is much documentation of this mother's rejection of her son and of the impairment of such basic functions as her ability to comfort him, to help him regulate his pattern of feeding, sleeping, elimination, and to make herself and the world interesting to him as the first step in the development of intimacy. His diapers were often drenched and smelled sour. Her need to nurture herself took precedence.

The periods of greatest detachment between mother and child occurred when the mother felt rejected or exploited by her husband, the baby's father. The father's interactions with the baby were sporadic and uneven.

Mother and son entered a lengthy observation and treatment program that was successful.

Perhaps it was preposterous to relate the relationship of a mother to her infant with our Joan, who was a young adult. But her regression back to pre-toilet-trained infancy, the preoccupation with eating, sleeping, and drenched, sour-smelling diapers, drew compelling comparisons. Had Joan undergone a similar rejection when her mother discovered that Herbert was involved in an affair? Did Margo displace all her anger and frustration on her daughter? Herbert had rejected not only Margo but Joan and the new baby as well.

It was not yet three months since Joan's arrival. Something galvanic was happening as Sandra poured more and more of herself into Joan. Where someone else would show signs of fatigue, Sandra arrived earlier than required each morning, often before daylight. Joan began to take in liquids, the supplement Ensure, and cereals. Her cheeks filled out, her face colored, and her weight increased by five pounds.

Words emerged from her silence, clumsy and disembodied, but words nevertheless She seldom spoke of herself in the first person singular, for example: "We love you, we need drink, we want bathroom, Joan says hello."

Soon Sandra and Joan were going outdoors and playing with a frisbee. At first Joan's legs would collapse after five minutes, and Sandra would help her back to the cottage. But Joan gained another five pounds, and the two began spending longer and longer periods of time outdoors. Another week passed and people began to say that things were looking better. Still, everybody kept their fingers crossed.

Then, one morning, Joan greeted Sandra with a loud lament: "I want my mother, my real mother!" Sandra had engineered Joan's nurturing, and Joan had found an "earth" mother. But what of her real mother? However good or bad, competent or incompetent, we professionals may believe a biologic mother to have been in bringing up her child, that basic and powerful desire for fusion between mother and child never leaves, probably not for a lifetime.

Sandra's mothering was strengthening Joan, filling a vacuum that had arrested her development virulently enough to keep her forever sick—unless corrected. But Joan now wanted her own mother. I decided to move with caution, and met with Margo Cadwallader soon after Joan's request.

Margo sat opposite me in my office. She was stiff backed and was wearing an expensively tailored dark flannel suit and white Reebok running shoes. She had recently transferred to her Buckingham office so as to make these impromptu visits easier.

"As you may be aware," I said, "Sandra Williams and the entire staff have been taking good care of Joan. Until now, your daughter hasn't expressed any desire to see anyone in the family. But it's been obvious that you have been one of the central characters in the rituals she performs. I need more answers, and I'm looking for your help."

"Fire away, Doctor."

"Your husband has been seeing another woman for seventeen years. Many wives in your situation would have left. Why are the two of you still together?" Margo shook her head rapidly and her hair fell in all directions over her face. "You must have some feelings about his lying, saying he was at academic or scientific conferences, knowing all along he was with his paramour."

Margo thought a while, then answered slowly and with deliberation, "Sometimes they did go to conferences." She paused briefly, then said, "I assume you want to know everything about me?"

"That would be nice," I answered.

"My father was fifty-two and mother forty-three when I was born, an only child. My childhood was lonely, and mother cold and distant. In fact, I was raised by an English nanny who took me to Wales every summer to visit with her family. I always looked forward to those long summers in Wales.

"They sent me to the best private schools, and I always got top grades; in fact, I always was in the honors program. Later, both in high school and college, I helped father in his small investment business.

"I met Herbert when we were both at Swarthmore. I

was overwhelmed and taken in by his large family. They were eccentric, but the home was always so lively. I vowed that when I had children, they would always be surrounded by lots of people."

Her face became lined with obvious turmoil. "I swear, we noticed nothing unusual about Joan during her childhood until she turned thirteen. She was precocious, and she had a photographic memory, especially for the written word. She finished Tolkien's *Lord of the Flies* when she was only nine, but other kids are just as bright." She seemed apologetic, guilty, as if she has discovered something that she hadn't known before. "I guess Joan did have trouble making friends, but so did I. We both won awards for scholarship, honor, deportment, general character, things like that."

Margo said that, as a child, she'd always been withdrawn, but her parents were much older. However, that wasn't true in Joan's case. "Herbert and I were always involved with everything around us."

"Joan would sit alone in the basement, sometimes for hours. And she began to lose interest in school, unable or unwilling to concentrate. When she lost her friends, she began to attach herself to Sarah's friends.

"My, my! How difficult it is to separate me from my daughter. You asked me about myself and I'm talking about her."

Her face showed a martyred determination, as though she were swallowing pails of pain, an expression I had seen on Joan's face. But Margo's eyes were angry, her lips pursed, her shoulders squared, in direct contrast to the softness that Joan's body would posture.

"Why do I stay with my husband? I don't know. I guess it is complicated. We were attached to each other. Probably each of us felt like the odd man out. His affair started after Joan was born. The woman was a graduate student then, supposedly very bright.

"I guess I've never been warm or affectionate, but how could I be with both my parents so cold. After our second child was born, I left with the girls and got an apartment. He begged me to come back and I did. But I had to protect myself and needed to do something with my life. I went to Wharton, got my accounting degree, and went to work. That's why the progression of baby sitters. I feel guilty about that, but I had to save myself. It's funny, but his affair is giving him something. We've drawn closer over the years."

Following this discussion, I immediately set up joint mother-daughter sessions for Joan and Margo.

2. Duet and Dichotomy

> My voices have forbidden me
> to confide them to anybody.
> And I will never reveal what
> they say, even though you cut
> my head off.
>
> Compte, *Joan of Arc*

Some mothers flow toward their child in need, like water toward a parched desert. Not Margo Cadwallader. She resembled a sculpture carved from frozen snow. Yet her eyes were riveted on Joan's every move. And her eyes betrayed her, for they were warm and loving.

The family had so much contact with the psychiatric establishment that the mother-daughter tie had become sterile, medicalized. A rapturous reunion took place when Margo reached out to bring her daughter close to her chest and held her there. It appeared that Margo's immediate task was to learn the difference between sickness and nonsickness, and to trust what she felt.

Joan allowed her mother to cuddle her, but she would not share her inner feelings, the emotions she was relearning, or learning for the first time. Sandra was helping her understand the basics of a relationship, and at times Joan would beam with inner pride at her newfound knowledge.

When Joan performed her rituals, Margo would become nervous and would lose patience. She was awed by her daughter's continuous cadence of obsessive thoughts, describing the process as "brilliant and creative." Both were wrapped up in failed relationships. And Margo was drinking, especially when her husband was with his paramour.

The estrangement between her parents probably started in Joan's formative years, for her first rituals were performed at two and one-half years of age when Sarah was born, and increased in volume and strength through the years.

I believed it was important to restore the healthy mother-infant ballet, to teach Margo a steadfast course of devotion, an attachment that would agglutinate as paper to the wall. Often, severely regressed patients will wait for their mothers to show change and will then learn from them; sometimes the reverse occurs.

The plan became easier when Herbert Cadwallader expressed outright hatred for Joan's illness and manifested repugnance even at being in the same room with his daughter.

On Tuesday and Friday afternoons, mother, daughter, the female houseparent, and, sometimes, I would meet for over an hour. Joan rarely spoke, and when she did it was in clipped sentences. After three months she had gained twenty pounds, no longer needed diapers, and had had her first menstrual period in two years. She had then developed an interest in books, reading *Little Women, The Hobbit,* and *The Secret Garden*. She also became fascinated by Joan of Arc.

But it was too early for optimism. In fact, penetration into the defense system of a mental illness can be compared to scaling the walls of a fortress with grappling hooks and ropes. There's a lot of trial and error.

I recalled Joan's excellent response to ECT (sixty percent improvement). Parents and doctors had been hopeful, but hope had faded as she once more regressed. The record showed an initial positive response to most of the different treatments, i.e., medication and behavioral interventions. Joan had defeated more than ten healers and the illness, whatever it was officially labeled, had continued unabated. Symptoms had returned more rigidly fixated, with the patient more omnipotent and distant, and everyone had feared for the future.

A dichotomy existed. She could show outward signs of contentment, breathing more easily and even smiling, while apparently harboring an inferno within.

The symptoms of psychosis peeled off like pockets of boiling steam, evidence of the volcano Joan carried inside. Periods of quietude existed, then the head-banging began again. To prevent her from cracking her skull open, we reapplied a football helmet. She sometimes squeezed her hands over her ears until hands and ears turned purple; yet she denied hearing voices.

"I'm listening to my own voice," she would say, rejecting help from others and devoting most of her day to getting the rituals "just right."

As huge waves of dread entered and left her body, she rejected Sandra. Then she refused food and water. After three days she had grown weaker.

By the fourth day, the scent of ketone emanating from Joan was as strong as the smell of diesel fuel. She had not urinated for two days. An ambulance was called. On the way to the hospital an intravenous saline/glucose solution was inserted into a vein. Once there, she was taken immediately to intensive care and strapped to a bed.

When the crisis began winding down, I was able to review how and why the case had changed so precipitously. Unable to stop a cataclysmic crisis as it heightened, Joan imagined enemies all around her. All voices, sounds, and thoughts were referred and not recognized as her own. It was she against the world. The stress was blowing her apart (implosion), and she would only say that she didn't feel very good.

Her psyche, in an attempt to reach inner peace, was going through this devastation in what nature believed was the most economic way for the human race, with no concern for her as an individual.

Many scholars have philosophized that it is the reaction to stress that is the real illness, and what is labeled mental illness or insanity is not a strange disease process but something simpler and more easily understood; the symptoms of the malady, hallucinations and delusions, have persisted so long, they might be considered nothing more than bad habit. But regardless of how the sickness is labeled, it remains a living nightmare. Any attempts at recovery create such discomfort that to try again and again requires too much energy. That is why there is such severe resistance to change in these unfortunates.

When Joan returned from the hospital, she was eating and drinking and appeared much calmer—and all this without medication. There was no visible reason not to renew the mother-daughter sessions.

During one session Joan stated, "I see myself as the little savage, Mary Lennox [from *The Secret Garden*]. She always had a sour face, and she was completely taken care of by maids. She heard voices but never had friends, except maybe Dickon, her dog. Mary was mean, you know. She kicked the servants frequently. But she never felt loved, and she dreamed of a secret garden where she could go. I guess I'm just like her."

Her mother and I were there to hear it all. But I listened not to the content so much as to the expression of the words. Now she spoke in whole sentences, no longer in the clipped Marx Brothers routine of Groucho and Chico feeding tip-of-the-tongue words to the mute Harpo. And she used the first person, not the third.

Suddenly she jumped up from her seat. "I must tell you something, Mother." She pointed wildly to me, her voice and expression agitated. Her body was shaking. "This man tried to feed me a baby bottle of milk. But I spit the milk out. He is an awful and dangerous man."

Margo Cadwallader also stood, indignation written on her face, hands on her hips, chin pointed out. "This is very upsetting. I sympathize with you, Joan. I wouldn't take a baby bottle, either, if he dared to try to give me one."

Neither outburst drew any response from me. Rather, I assumed a tutorial role, believing it important to remind both of them that Joan had just lived through two alluvion crises that could have ended her life. No one could predict whether there would be a third, but insight and understanding could reduce the pain and serve as a deterrent. Most adolescents do not reflect or analyze what has happened yesterday. Most see each new day as a new life; most are interested in neither the past nor the future.

"You spend your life, lady," I said to Joan, "protecting yourself with outmoded defenses, whether they be smashing your head or refusing to eat or drink. Maybe as a child, they got you attention. But now you're grown up. These defenses alienate you from people. So you remain weak and vulnerable. You constantly struggle against nerve-wracking emotions. You always feel that you will disappear, disintegrate. That's why the busywork, the rituals, trying to get them perfect. When that doesn't work, you pulverize a window, stop eating, or freeze into catatonia. What are you going to do next?"

There was no answer.

The weekly sessions continued. I flung a barrage of questions and new ideas at her, asking one day why she had submitted to all the forms of treatment.

"You don't know," she replied, "how impossible it is not to be able to tell the difference between feelings and ideas. My emotions have been so married to the rituals that I couldn't trust what I felt."

This young woman was obviously of superior intellect, and she carried herself with dignity. There were other positive aspects of her personality that could be mobilized for the fight still ahead. For example, she had strong beliefs about injustice and inequality.

The following months were relatively happy. She and her mother continued to find common ground. When they talked openly, the mother's idealization of the illness was not as strong as it had been.

A carefree, impish side of Joan's personality surfaced with spurts of sudden abandon, and she relinquished the solemn practice of the rituals. She might display a wide-eyed, seraphic smile as she bunny-hopped around the room repeating, "Love, love, love." Her mother never accepted this behavior and insisted that the pupils of Joan's eyes tended to dilate during these exhibitions. Did she believe that her daughter suffered from a form of epilepsy? Margo was never happy to hear that her daughter often grabbed food from the table during dinner, and that it ended up plastered to the ceiling.

The mother-daughter sessions sometimes got bogged down, and the team sought a way to ease the father into the therapy. Although he was interested, he reminded us many times of his demanding teaching schedule and research commitments. The visits, therefore, had to be impromptu.

And that they were. He tended to show up at the unit

at odd hours, sometimes before seven in the morning, sometimes late at night when Joan was in bed. Because he always seemed rushed for time, looking constantly at his watch, his visits were mostly unproductive, nonverbal, and icy. Once in a while Joan would let him slip a blanket over her or place an arm around her shoulders.

One day, while a straightjacketed Joan sat next to her father, his arm around her, Margo inadvertently walked in. Her husband jumped up, thus ending a tender father-daughter moment. Margo glared at her husband with circles of hate. After neutralizing him, she turned to Joan.

"What happened? You were perfectly fine when I talked to you on the phone last night."

"I wasn't so fine," Joan retorted. "That's how much you really know me. This whole family is very screwed up, Mom. Do something for yourself. Treat yourself to a good therapist. It might help." An indignant Margo looked at her husband and held eye contact before saying, "I don't need it. I won't go."

Herbert rose and with true Victorian chivalry exclaimed, "My wife is the most well-adjusted, competent person I ever met." After a moment of reflective silence, he came out with, "Maybe I put her on a pedestal. These two women are very much alike. They are both martyrs who, underneath, are omnipotent and angry."

Margo diffused the tension quickly. Turning to Joan, she said, "You're getting the chance to grow up I never had. Don't throw it away."

Following that incident, Margo stopped in at the unit every day after work, sometimes staying for dinner. Despite the negatives, a new bond was growing between them.

Herbert often hypothesized that the illness had "biologic roots." In answer, Margo would spin a web of maternal protection around her daughter.

"Remember," Herbert once said, "how she would refuse dinner and hole up in her room. I bet she wasn't more than five or six. I know she was hiding, probably performing those rituals of hers. It's in her genes."

"That's plain nonsense," Margo exclaimed, her nostrils flaring. "If you were honest, you'd remember all the bickering and fighting going on in this house, especially at dinner."

The two never agreed on anything; the everpresent shadow of the other woman permeated the room.

Mother-daughter sessions continued twice a week. Joan's clipped manner of speech, devoid of emotion, also continued. But no longer did she repeat, "Love, love, Mother, Father."

Margo enjoyed these sessions, possibly gaining more strength from them than did her daughter. She induced Herbert to agree to bring Joan to Block Island, where the family spent summers at grandmother's bungalow estate. But a full-sized mother doll, which Sandra and Joan had stuffed with newspapers and started to sew after Margo had lain on the floor and allowed herself to be traced for the pattern, ended up half finished in a dark corner behind a couch, like a human fetus thrown into a garbage can. It was decided that Joan would not make the trip until this doll was finished. Joan's reaction to this task was a series of binding rituals, magical hand gestures, and accusatory whining and shouting that always ended in wailings of "I want to go home."

The plane was to leave Philadelphia International Airport the next morning. Under the canopy of family ceremony, houseparents and other family assistants who worked with Joan helped her finish the doll, giving birth to a nameless, faceless textile. Breathing life into this invertebrate by adding eyes, a mouth, ears, hair, and clothes, would have to wait. The great burst of cooperative energy shattered Joan's wishy-washy paralysis and catatonic lethargy. She flew to Block Island with her father.

When she returned, she appeared radiant and ebullient. I offered her a session without her mother present, and she agreed, provided that Sandra could be there.

She spoke in full sentences and seemed self-assured, so much so that I almost wondered if she was the same person who had left.

"I have a mission," she said, "a burning desire in the pit of my stomach. I must help people who are hurting. I want to open up, let more in, and that's frightening. When I do, the rituals become more punitive. It's confusing; these rituals are mixed with my own feelings. Sometimes they

93

feel like a friend. I believe my mother and sister will die if I stop the rituals. Also, I'm using obscenities and that was never me."

Was she beginning to show signs of the unmitigated anger that can escape once obsessions no longer work?

The idea of admitting father into the therapeutic inner sanctum arose again after the successful trip to Block Island. Would Joan have been so cooperative if Margo had gone with her? Events to follow would answer the question.

3. Antidepressants and Tigers

Margo had urged her daughter to use Prozac despite Joan's contention that the drug had produced insipid results during her previous hospital stay. While Joan was at The Clinic, the makers of the drug sponsored a staff luncheon to demonstrate the efficiency of their product. Margo attended the luncheon and, uplifted by the speakers' persuasive speech, again approached her daughter about trying the medication.

Sensing the drama about to unfold, I believed some play- acting was in order. I told Joan that, according to the law, no authority can force a patient to take medication against his or her will. However, since it was her mother making the request, Joan would have to write out her reasons for refusal and her mother would have to sign that document.

At the kitchen table, Joan thoughtfully listed her reasons for refusing to take the drug. Then she pushed the paper across the table to her mother who sat opposite her.

"This is ridiculous, a farce!" her mother shouted and tossed the paper to the floor without reading the contents.

Joan bolted from her chair over to her mother and began to pummel her mother's face with her fists. Then she fell to the floor shouting, "Sarah, I love you, I love you, Sarah."

The visibly shaken Margo, her face reddened and bleeding, left the unit quickly, bumping into her husband, who coincidentally had just stopped by for a visit and had witnessed the fight from outside the unit entrance.

Margo and Herbert had begun to see a change in Joan; they agreed she appeared to be stronger, even strong enough to spend Saturday evenings at home. On one such occasion, Joan and her mother visited Margo's invalid mother in Malvern.

The parents complained about the bills, wanting to omit the one-on-one care Joan still needed.

"From my experience," I said, as they sat in my office, "I would bet the extra care your daughter receives will vitalize her and fill her with a new self-reliance, and probably save you money later."

They listened politely but with obvious disbelief. They did not especially value my remarks—that is, until Sandra's automobile accident.

One night, Sandra worked late preparing Joan for bed. Since Joan was no longer incontinent, rubber sheeting was not needed. Bathing and powdering Joan, she pulled the covers over her, kissed her good night, and left in her ten-year-old Cadillac for her drive home to North Philadelphia.

That trip was ill-fated. The Cadillac was rammed broadside. Sandra's head cracked the windshield, her body jolted and jammed beneath the collapsed dashboard. When extricated, she was taken to the nearest hospital where x-rays revealed two broken legs and a fractured pelvis. She went home in a body cast, to be cared for by her mother and her aunt.

Though Sandra's presence was greatly missed at the unit, the first session with Joan and her parents could not be delayed. Herbert was obsessed with the payments for extra care, and his anxiety filtered through to his wife at every session. Now was the time to face the issues head on.

"How is your daughter doing?" I asked one Friday afternoon after Herbert agreed to join us. (How I wished Sandra were there!)

"She seems more in control, and her visits home are without much incident," he said. "But she keeps her distance emotionally. I've been thinking that maybe she should begin to work, earn some money, even volunteer at a hospital."

But Joan was on top of this remark quicker than a terrier on a bone. "Why do you think I'm so exhausted all the time? I am working full time, twenty-four hours a day, doing rituals. Doing them just right is extremely difficult. I'd like to see you do it."

Sensing a potential explosion, Margo turned to her husband. "You speak of Joan's difficulty negotiating space. Have you ever noticed how phobic I am? Probably not. I avoid going to a lot of places. You bicycle twenty-five, thirty miles just for fun. How could you understand anybody struggling just to go around corners?"

Looking at me, the professor said, "She and I first started to date when we were eighteen. I never knew she was phobic."

Joan added, "Remember when Elsie [Joan's roommate and sister patient] came to spend the night with me last weekend? Well, she felt very strange in that house. Nobody in our house ever hugs anybody."

There was a question that Herbert had to answer, and now was as good as any time. I asked, "Why did you tell Joan of your affair, and not tell Sarah?"

Herbert moved his gangly limbs but didn't answer. That ended the session, and the parents left in separate cars. Joan sat quietly, with stiffened back, hands folded politely on her lap. She moved her mouth rhythmically, apparently in deep concentration. Later she confided she was performing rituals that, like prayers or recitations, didn't need acting out.

It was during times like this that Joan would collapse in Sandra's arms. But there was no Sandra, and there wouldn't be for at least three months.

Joan tried to confide in Sandra's replacement, but the regression that occurred after Sandra's leaving was, like a comet entering the atmosphere, unstoppable, until finally it hit the steel frame that housed the illness, exposing it so that the illness could virtually be seen with the naked eye, flourishing like a colony of ants.

I recalled to Joan the past nine months. "Remember when you crashed through the window? Remember the dehydration and the hospital? What about the voices?"

She didn't answer.

"You aren't Joan of Arc and I'm not the Inquisitor

Cauchon, so please, let's try to talk about some things."

I recalled silently words from Joan of Arc's personal diary. "Do you still believe your voices are St. Marguerite and St. Catherine?" Cauchon asked Joan. "Yes," Joan replied, "and they come from God." Joan of Arc knew that this statement, along with the repudiation of her confession, would doom her to fire. "I would rather do my penance all at once," she said. "I cannot endure captivity any longer."

If our Joan considered herself courageous, it wasn't visible. The closest she came to answering questions was to drop her shoulder-length hair in front of her face, a dramatic gesture that signified her desire to be left alone. She was a mistress of the turnoff, and most people would leave her alone and go on to someone more stimulating.

Then again, she might change the subject through silence, subtlety creating a conversational void so that others began to talk for her and make decisions for her.

"I can egg people on," she once said. Her parents and her doctors must have had to suppress much frustration and anger. Did these interactions account for her being subjected to electric shock treatment? I wondered.

Another family session was scheduled for Friday, one week hence. Tuesday afternoons still belonged to Joan and her mother.

The week passed quickly. Surprisingly, there was no violent acting out, so it was decided to ferret out Herbert's longstanding love affair. It was still my belief that his uninhibited pursuit of the affair had long ago isolated Margo, and the wounded mother could have gone down the line, as in a brace of dominoes, turning her resentment against her oldest daughter. Trapped inside a steel cage, Joan's rapidly souring personality had no escape. Herbert was no help, choosing to go outside the family to meet his emotional needs with blatant disregard for the consequences.

Though the sessions with mother and daughter were becoming more fruitful, the sessions with father along had lately served as a dumping station for both personal and family garbage.

One Tuesday Joan arrived with a large egg-shaped hematoma clearly visible on the right occipital part of her head.

"I forgot to do the regular rituals before I went to sleep last night. I awoke about four in the morning to bang my head. I must do these rituals every morning. If I don't, the sun won't rise. I must have done something right. See how beautiful it is outside now?"

To her mother she said, "I've been remembering back to when I was three, to that New Year's Eve. It was awful. You were so sad. Remember all the whiskey? It made you so strange. Dad wasn't there. I didn't know it then, but he was with his girl friend. I wanted to help you so much, but I didn't know how. So I developed magic. I would say numbers under my breath, and repeat them. You know, someday I might want to have children, but I'm afraid I'll end up like you."

On Friday Herbert came into the meeting sporting an accusatory affectation. He was obviously hurt by Joan's defiant attack during the previous session and by her refusal to accept his ride back from her last visit home. Looking intently at his daughter, he opened the session by asking, "Why don't you want to come home? You never ask anymore."

Joan, sitting with back straight, hands folded in a perpendicular lap, and feet planted on the floor, replied, "Of course I like to come home. But there are times when it is more healthful to stay here on a weekend."

Margo, in her chair, had become agitated, flitting her eyes and moving her body back and forth.

Herbert, his voice dripping sarcasm, said, "Maybe you do like it better here."

"No, that's not it. But it may be good for me at times to stay here on a weekend."

Herbert squared his shoulders and tensed his neck. "You're certainly not like me. I can make decisions."

Margo weakened the fiery brew with tepid water and interjected, "I'm the one who can't make decisions."

I looked at all three of them. "Why is everybody afraid to tell Sarah, who is fifteen now, about this other woman and his previous affairs?"

It was Joan who broke the confirming silence. "Sarah and I talk a lot. She is the only one I trust. I've never told her, but I think she suspects the truth."

I noticed that Herbert's shirt collar was soaked with perspiration. It appeared he would never be able to tell his youngest daughter the truth.

Joan faced him squarely. "You keep pressuring me to come home. What do you want? Do you want this thing to start all over again? Neither of you believe that I will ever be well. I'm going to stay here until I'm ready for college."

Herbert's tone was far from placating. "If I didn't have this damn expense, I could get myself a boat, go sailing, relax."

"What are we going to do about telling Sarah?" I asked again.

Margo spoke up. "She's coming home next week. Maybe she could come with us to a session. I'll let you know in a few days."

The family requested a meeting for the following Thursday instead of Friday, since they were going on a ski trip—that is, all of them except Joan. Sarah would be able to attend the session. She had visited her sister several times, and they had spoken frequently on the phone.

As the meeting began, both parents were extremely anxious. Herbert's face was reddish purple, his scalp watering profusely.

"Sarah," he began, "I've never had the guts to tell you something." His eyes fell to Sarah's feet. "I believe you're old enough to know the truth. I've been seeing another woman for many years, actually. It...it started soon after you were born."

Then Sarah looked directly into her father's eyes. "I often wondered why there was such silence in that house, why the family had become so dysfunctional. You are some big bastard for laying this all on my sister."

A sound of swirling saliva came from her mouth. She went on. "I blame myself, but the only way I could react to the nightmare at home was to get away to school. That's why I had so many friends. I was safe at boarding school and now, at college."

Herbert's tone became pleading. "Please, I want to end this lousy affair now. I've wanted to for five years but I'm too weak. I need the family's help."

He looked first at Sarah, then Joan, then his wife. It appeared he was falling deeper into a sandpit even as he tried to extricate himself. His wife, having reached equanimity and sufferance with the arrangement, for whatever reason, was not about to throw him a ladder.

After the session, Joan's ritual performances began to taper off, but the empty spaces and dark holes produced by the cessation of rituals created great anxiety within her. She had lost so much of her life to illness that, without her litany, she was left naked. During these long periods of hesitation and doubt, and the waning of the strong belief system, it was Margo who became alive. Margo's mission now was to cure her daughter.

Joan passed her GED and, as in the past, called her sister to reinforce her desire to go to college.

Herbert's revelation had not caused Sarah to break down; the family's fears had been unwarranted. But my hopes that the revelation would free Joan of all symptoms were far from realized, and there occurred little shift in the family dynamics.

At the next session Herbert, with a new boldness, claimed that all Sarah needed now was a boyfriend. Margo said nothing, and Joan harangued her mother for not protecting Sarah. Disgusted with her father's insensitivity, she cried out, "If you don't stop picking on my sister, the next time I'm home I'll spill a bottle of Coke all over your computer."

Herbert fell silent because he knew she would do it. His nightly routine was to escape to his study and play computer games. Sometimes Margo never even knew he was home.

Neighboring The Clinic was a small college. Joan, although not completely free of symptoms, voiced a desire to attend one course there. Because Sandra remained on disability, and other staffers were needed in the units, she would have to traverse the campus unattended. Still, she was adamant in her wish to attend class.

Every Tuesday at six-thirty, Joan appeared for Basic English, sitting quietly in the last row, taking what notes she could between the silent ritualism of number mazing and puzzle solving. Only occasionally would she shout out some indistinguishable phrase. When this happened, the lecturer would stop, and all eyes would turn to Joan. She would beg forgiveness for disrupting the class, saying that she suffered from Tourette's syndrome. An uncontrollable neurological tic is more acceptable to the general population than a mysterious mental illness.

Joan fumbled her way through the English course and began to look for other ways to spend time away from The Clinic. I think she may have believed that Sandra had abandoned her and was not really recuperating at home, with both feet elevated and stretched by pulleys. Joan's venturing from The Clinic seemed to be a search for Sandra just as a child might undertake a quest for a biologic mother who had given her up for adoption.

Summer neared and Joan came to me one day to say, "I want to volunteer some time at the YMCA. I think I have something to give little kids."

She began to work with the children at the Y, but one morning she disappeared during lunch break. Alarmed, the Y called The Clinic. Several of our people combed the woods adjacent to the Y and found Joan sitting in the lotus position under a large oak tree, chanting a mantra designed for "escape and freedom."

Until now, Joan had been working out her conflicts with humans. But, like many sensitive and shy people, she favored animals.

One day Herbert announced that he, Margo, and Sarah would be taking part in a sailing regatta on Block Island.

"What are you doing with Trusty?" Joan wanted to know.

Trusty was the family dog, a long-legged, short-haired, mud-colored mongrel of medium size who was a mix of shepherd, retriever, and other breeds. A former stray, he was a nervous dog.

"He'll be going to his favorite kennel," Herbert replied. "You know where he'll be."

Thus began what was probably the greatest crisis of Joan's treatment.

Joan had always displayed an intense love for Trusty. Now she conceived a special ritual where she would spend a complete day jumping off a sailboat moving through deep water, using every stroke possible to swim to shore. The water would have to be very cold with high swells. The greater the ordeal, the more she would prove her love for Trusty.

In a frenzy, Joan spent three and a half frantic hours "getting the ritual just right." Drooling with saliva and constantly licking her lips, she developed a headache from concentration. But nothing worked.

She then ran to a cinder-block wall and, with the force of a wrecker, banged her head repeatedly against it. It took six powerful men to restrain her and end her self-massacre. After the bleeding was contained and her wounds sutured, she was asked, "Why?"

"I must smash my head, crack my skull to the point of death, to prove to Trusty that I love him."

She continued to obsess about Trusty being in "that awful, bare, cold cell." It was as though she identified with Trusty, feeling unwanted and not worthy of a trip with the family. Refusing medication, pacing day and night, she was placed on suicide watch.

Into the third day, the treatment team met and planned an end to the crisis. A team member accompanied Joan to the kennel, freed Trusty, and brought him to the unit. Dog and young woman then comforted and cared for each other. That is, until a staff member carelessly left a door open and Trusty bolted out. But sometime later, the dog was lured by the smell of hot dogs to another unit's outdoor grill. After eating everything in sight, he returned home to Joan who fed, exercised, and generally cared for him until the family returned. Thus a potentially powerful disaster was averted.

After this incident Joan became determined to join the family on their next journey—a fishing trip to northern Ontario. She was invited, and she successfully managed the trip. Upon her return she announced that her many hospitalizations would come to an end. Rumors were circulating throughout the community about my upcoming sabbatical. Joan resolved to leave inpatient care at the same time.

"I'm ready for a freer and less structured environment," she said to me one day. "But I can't live at home. You know about the awful fights when I go home for weekends."

It was Herbert who pressed for her discharge, but he wished her to live at home where she and her mother would keep each other company. This way, he could continue to see his paramour in complete family silence.

Margo's reaction to Joan's individuation was two-pronged: She was happy for her daughter's attempt at separation but also angry because, with Joan not at home, she would have to face Herbert "eyeball to eyeball."

Joan, ignoring her father's wishes, left for a transitional boarding home within walking distance of the college. She continued under-the-breath rituals, but the days of the "grand display"—head banging, catatonia, life-and-death urgency —were gone.

She continued to spend some weekends with her former roommate at The Clinic. Together they had made the journey from insanity and now were bonded in a relationship based on trial and turmoil.

Joan spoke to me of enrolling for full course credit. "I don't care what grades I get. I'm going for therapeutic reasons."

Sitting across from her, seeing her sit quietly, bespectacled and bookish, I recalled earlier days when her face had been full of agony, gloom, horror, and confusion.

Joan is no longer my patient, but I hear about her happenings. She is attending college, driving her own car, working part time in a coffee shop, and seeing a young man who is a fellow student. Her parents are still together, with no change in their relationship.

Postscript

One morning I awoke wondering what reason I had for comparing Joan to the Maid of Orleans. And did it work?

Those who revere the ancient Joan might be offended and rightfully so. As the Sieur de Compte said on his eightieth birthday, "I was her page and secretary. I was with her from the beginning to the end. I came to comprehend and recognize her for what she was—the most noble life ever born into this world save One."

Joan of Arc came from humble peasant stock, Joan Cadwallader from the privileged classes. But both were shy and innocent in childhood and, even as they matured into adulthood, remained unaware and untrained in the ways of the world.

Joan of Arc was nicknamed "the Bashful" by her playmates; Joan Cadwallader's only playmates were her stuffed animals and her dog, Trusty.

Both developed into recalcitrant visionaries whose personal lives were unimportant to them. Ancient Joan was fiercely loyal to her nation, while modern Joan remained steadfastly faithful to her family.

Both professed to abhor violence yet self-righteously employed violence in the service of a holy mission.

Both were brave. Legend has it the Maid of Orleans once tamed a madman. Modern Joan showed a brief period of bravery and rebellion, even leadership, in her own crusade, until the illness overwhelmed her. She was also brave in her personal journey to overcome her illness. Medicine and numerous doctors had failed her. She always has carried a disdain for both.

Both Joans carried noble beauty and grace. Yet they were strikingly different in accomplishment. "Joan of Arc, a mere child in years, seventeen when she led France in victory, turning back the tide of the Hundred Years War, crowning the French king, the same king who stood indifferently by while French priests took the noble child...and burned her alive at the stake."

Joan Cadwallader, during her illness, was unable to negotiate either time or her own space in everyday living. No one listened when she gave advice because she set such a poor example. She was obsessed with her inner evil. When voices spoke of her baseness, she succumbed. With little self worth, she easily became a doctor's experiment.

Joan of Arc was defiled and dishonored, treated as a common criminal, tortured by persecutors. She died a martyr. "They are very dear to me, my voices," she said at the stake, as pitchy smoke swirled around her and red flashes of flame licked at her legs. "My voices have never lied to me."

It is said that Joan went to her death with her head raised toward the heavens, listening to the voice of God. It was a quarter of a century later (1431) before she went through the process of Rehabilitation. Records of the trial, martyrdom, and sainthood are preserved in the National Archives of France.

Joan Cadwallader's rehabilitation may also take twenty-five years, but maybe not. Whatever one may think, she is alive and is learning more and more about life and love. (I've been told she recently received a masters degree in literature, was working, and had a more-than-casual friendship with a young man).

She has never admitted to being crazy, only to going through a transfiguration. Because of human failures in what was, for a long time, a perfect system—her mental illness—she was able to escape immolation.

Chapter IV
In a Wild State

1. Homeless

This next story may seem unconnected to the previous three, but homelessness is one of our greatest social blights and a breeding ground for disease and mental illness. In fact, it is estimated there are six to seven thousand men and women living on the streets of New York alone, although advocates for the homeless claim many more. As far as disease goes, sixty-two percent of men in a homeless shelter are HIV-positive, and fifty percent have tuberculosis, according to *New York* magazine. Thousands of the homeless are sick and dying. What's more, they are passing their diseases on to us.

This story begins in Manhattan on a winter night when temperatures had plummeted to the single digits. The owner and manager of Mr. G's Friendly Market was preparing to close the store early, as the bad weather brought in few customers. Reaching for the safety bolt to secure the front door, he saw a familiar sight under the store's safety lights.

"Come in, Max," he said, "it's freezing out there."

The man called Max was a pitiable sight. Leaning on a broomstick in the darkened shadows of the building, he was bone thin and was wrapped in burlap, with a matching cape around his shoulders. There wasn't a comb on the market that could have penetrated his long, matted hair, and his sludgy beard bore remnants of his last meager meal. He wore no shoes on his crusted, scaled, and calloused feet. His rheumy eyes darted to and fro, possibly in fear, possibly in wonder.

"Where were you last night, Max?" the storekeeper

asked, hoping to begin a conversation with the man.

"Why do you ask?" Max replied. His tone was clipped, flat, and barely audible, and his facial expression mournfully deadpan.

Attempting to wisecrack with the unfortunate wretch before leaving for the night, the storekeeper said, "Max, with all this food here, you can have a feast. Tomorrow, I'll come in and see a big, fat Buddha sitting here." He attempted to poke Max's shoulder playfully, but Max cringed from the overture.

The proprietor gave up, not wanting to pry into the thoughts of another man. Even derelict prophets deserved their privacy.

"Well anyway, you can sweep the floor, Max. And make sure you help yourself to anything you want to eat. I'll see you in the morning." The storekeeper already knew what the ragamuffin would select: one, maybe two, plain yogurts, one-half to one pint of milk, a dozen peanuts. After this sparse meal Max would spread his burlap cover on the concrete floor, staying awake for hours in a tight, hunched position, alert for the attack he always expected.

The storekeeper wondered whether Max ever bathed. He certainly had no body odor. Did he ever use the toilet? The storekeeper saw no clues. But when he opened the Ninth Avenue shop in the morning, he knew he would find his guest bare-chested, head thrown back, arms and hands and palms outspread, as if drenching himself in the sun's rays.

Was this position an outward manifestation of some strange, silent prayer? Was this man a mere vagabond, or could he be a saint, or even a prophet from some mysterious religion?

No one was sure. But it was known that Max went to Mr. G's Market only in extremely bad weather or when the environs of his territory—two square blocks between Sixty-third and Sixty-fourth streets between Ninth and Tenth avenues—became especially ominous.

For it was these streets, inhabited twenty-four hours a day by prostitutes and their pimps conducting illicit commerce in sex and drugs, that had become Max's neighborhood. And in a narrow alley between two rundown brownstones that housed the city's most recent flow of immigrants from Peru and the Yucatan, Max made his home. Perhaps the large shipping crate he used as shelter had once harbored an upright piano or a commercial refrigerator. Now it contained mangled old blankets, soiled clothing, and piles of indispensable burlap, Max's only claim to domestic life.

One morning, about two o'clock, a homeless wino wandered into Max's alley, crawled inside his cardboard home, and fell asleep. When he awoke and saw Max, he feared for his life and started biting and flailing his newly found roommate. Blood spilled, and the screams and other strange sounds alarmed the Peruvians, who called the police. Both men were taken to Bellevue Hospital in a city ambulance.

On a quiet Saturday afternoon, more than a year later and many miles away, I sat at my desk in The Clinic's administration building, attempting to catch up on overdue paperwork. When the phone rang, I lifted the receiver to hear the cultivated voice of a middle-aged woman who must certainly have spent some part of her life in the theater.

"Dr. Honig, I hope? Yes, well am I happy to be speaking with you! I have a magazine article about you in front of me that is almost twenty years old. I don't know why I waited so long. My God! Suppose it is too late! Please, Dr. Honig, I am calling about my son. He's been given up for hopeless by the best doctors. I am frantic, frantic."

With hardly a pause, she went on. "They transferred him from Bellevue a year ago. He's been on the ward under court order all this time. He refuses voluntary hospitalization. Darling, it's a long story. How can a mother face such a verdict about her son? He's brilliant, talented, beautiful inside. A doctor, same as you. Please, Dr. Honig, may I bring him to see you?"

She described her son's problem with maternal energy and theatrical verve. But I needed little convincing after hearing the first thrust of information. The more I heard, the more fascinated I became.

His name was Maxwell Cowen, M.D. He had been a dashing psychiatrist who had graduated in the upper ten percent of his class at Downstate Medical College; he was also a writer and a pianist, and had shown promise as a classical composer.

The young Dr. Cowen had established quite a reputation at the city-run Free Psychiatry Clinic at Eleventh Avenue and Fifty-fourth Street. He had been recognized as a sensitive, persistent, and patient therapist, especially attuned to the problems of the underprivileged. In fact, the clinic's other therapists referred their most recalcitrant, angry, rebellious adolescent patients to Dr. Cowen; he understood them, and they understood him. Whole street gangs, one member referred by another, had been seen entering his office.

His patients had shared his personal life. He spent many weekends either at Jones Beach or in the Poconos, and always one of his young patients went with him. It was not unusual to see his red MG sports coupe, with top down regardless of the weather, racing along the West Side Drive toward the George Washington Bridge, with an adolescent in the passenger seat.

In his professional life he had been no less persistent. Three evenings a week Dr. Cowen had attended the William Allison White Institute for Psychoanalysis as a candidate in psychoanalytic diploma. Here he garnered respect from colleagues and teachers alike. In his last year at the Institute, he had agonized over whether to remain at the public clinic, grossly underpaid for long hours, or to enter private practice where the fees were higher and demands much lower.

One of Dr. Cowen's control cases was a thirty-year-old male schoolteacher obsessed with the delusional belief that he had contracted tuberculosis. Physical and medical examinations, including workups and x-rays, had been performed and analyzed. All of these tests proved negative for tuberculosis or other infections. His patient's problem was not physical.

Dr. Cowen's supervisor did not believe medication would diminish this man's delusionary beliefs. So Dr. Cowen made the exhausting and mentally draining commitment to convince his patient the illness was emotional. But during this five-days-a-week ordeal, a rare and peculiar phenomenon took place: the doctor "contracted" the same delusionary "disease" suffered by his patient.

His rational physician's mind told him that to contract tuberculosis from another person requires prolonged close contact, even to the point of living with the person. Still, his emotional makeup precluded accepting this logic.

He told no one of his suspicions—not his supervisor, not his colleagues, not even the patient himself. He grew to believe he had been inescapably contaminated. He became cautious about the clothing he wore, even to the point of banishing his cherished Palm Beach and Calvin Klein suits to a distant corner of his closet.

In a panic one day, he visited his mother. She realized he wasn't "well" and, hiding the fear that her son's world (and, therefore, hers as well), was crumbling around them, she suggested that he see his former analyst. Maxwell did this but quit after two sessions.

From there, matters deteriorated quickly. Maxwell dropped out of the clinic, abandoned his sports car after it stalled in the middle of Eighth Avenue, and eventually went into seclusion inside his apartment.

Max assured his mother during regular phone calls that he was "fine." But he soon stopped calling, and he refused to answer incoming calls. His mother, frantic with worry, burst into his apartment one day to find her son sitting serenely in the lotus position. Clad only in undershorts, his lips parched from dehydration, he looked like a starved Mahatma Gandhi.

She made arrangements for his immediate hospitalization at an elegant and respected psychiatric institution New York City. After a three-month stay with treatment that was mainly medication, Max was discharged. He returned to his apartment but not for long; after several homeless years he was taken to Bellevue.

I assured Mrs. Cowen that I welcomed the opportunity to help her son. Since a bed would be available the following week, I suggested she have his doctor call me as soon as possible.

The call from Max's treating physician left me more involved, but also agitated.

"He's difficult, arrogant, hidden," the doctor told

me. "We can't keep him here any longer because he isn't progressing. He takes no initiative or responsibility for his own care, and that, Dr. Honig, is a poor prognostic indicator. I could summarize the case by saying: Maxwell Cowen is too afraid to let anyone tell him what to do, he hates to hear anything unpleasant, he wants to do whatever damn well pleases him, and he expects other people to accept him the way he is. He believes no one can help him. He clings to what he calls his 'image.'

"You know, Doc," the hospital doctor continued, "Max is stuck inside his psychosis. There's been no evidence of change in his system, and that's one of *his* words. In my opinion, it's a complicated delusional system. One of his big beliefs is fear of contamination. He's like a lizard changing colors, inventing a delusion to fit every emotional crisis. He's passive aggressive on the ward, refusing to bathe and change his clothes. To tell the truth, he's a hell of a pain in the ass, and a big drain on our nursing staff. We all want him out."

I thanked the doctor for his honest appraisal of Max's condition and hung up the phone, wondering what the hell I had let myself in for.

Maxwell and his mother appeared in The Clinic's waiting room at ten-thirty on Monday. The contrast between them could not have been more stark. Mrs. Cowen appeared poised, her every gesture perfectly timed and executed as though rehearsed, and her words formed like polished marble and delivered with Shakespearian panache. She was superbly dressed in gray, white, and variations of dusk. She sat there in the twilight of her career, an aging diva, an elegant, straight-backed Victoria Regina, with both hands clasping a silver-headed walking stick.

Her son was not without his own sense of theatrics. Sitting in the corner of the room, passive and detached, he presented a strikingly unappealing picture: matted hair and beard, the bristles of his upper lip soiled with particles of food, nasal drippings, saliva, and other seasonings and weavings that fastened upper and lower lip together over a severely hidden mouth.

Maxwell's back was painfully curved, his head set

so far to the rear that his chest swayed concavely. Seen close up, his neck appeared scrawny; but from a distance it was completely concealed between two humps of shoulders drawn high, as though to shelter the neck's vulnerability. From these humps dangled his arms and hands. His fingers ended in curved nails, more than an inch long, which resembled the talons of a bird of prey.

He wore a cut-out yellow shirt and burlap sack remnants, which included a wraparound cape with "Jack Frost Sugar" printed in blue and a formerly white bag showing "XXX" and "Pillsbury Flour" printed in red.

His bare feet were encrusted with hardened dirt. He, too, carried a walking stick: a stave of wood from a tree branch. I wondered how many of New York's street-wise teenagers had felt the swish of this stick in response to their taunting remarks.

After acquainting me with the details of their arrival, and with nary a glance at her son, Mrs. Cowen said, "Max, say hello to the good doctor."

Max had other ideas. From his chair in the far corner of the room he regarded me with a cold stare. His lips quivered and his tongue moved. Such movements are often seen in chronic brain syndrome, organic dementia, syphilis, Korsakoff psychosis, presenile cerebral arteriosclerosis, and even irreversible brain damage gone unrecognized and undiagnosed. His face showed visible anguish. He looked much older than thirty-two.

Mrs. Cowen ignored her son's bad manners and opened a black leather briefcase. "Come, doctor, look at these records." Placing a sheaf of papers on my desk, she said, "Yes, I know what you're thinking. He does look awful, but his neurological workup was normal."

Her regal hands encircled the walking stick. "Somehow, somewhere, Doctor, I believe there is hope."

She raised a delicate silk handkerchief to brush away sudden tears, but quickly regained her composure. "It's been a tiring day, Doctor, and who knows when I'll be here again. So I must give you some background."

She went on to describe Max's earliest days. He had been born healthy. In a tone of abject apology, she explained that clock feeding was then in vogue and mothers usually let their babies cry between feedings. Max would often cry himself to sleep, and she would have to wake him to force him to suck.

"Now I know it was wrong," she said, pausing briefly, and in her face I saw the pain of regret. "Now I fear this action of mine caused Max's strange food problems."

Nevertheless, Max was a happy child, she said. "And there was never a more loved nor precious child. His development was rapid: he walked and talked before most children, and toilet-trained himself. He adored his father, and although he loved me, he truthfully loved being with his father more. But I was content to stay in the background, watching my little boy build a relationship with the man-father."

Max's father, it seemed, had been an often-unemployed set designer. He and little Max would play miniature golf, pitch and putt, or pursue other male forms of recreation. But all this collapsed when Max's father fell in love with another woman. Mrs. Cowen was in the hospital giving birth to their daughter when her husband decided to abandon the family.

"It was a ghastly situation," she said, obviously reliving the memory. "Max was four and a half at the time. His father tried to explain things to him, but the trauma must have been staggering. I'd had no inkling whatsoever of his intentions. Suddenly there was a newborn baby in a house that reeled with overwhelming emotional chaos."

She paused. "Should I continue, Doctor, while my son listens to all this?"

I looked again at Maxwell. He sat, motionless, staring. I nodded and she went on.

"Even with the new baby, I tried never to deprive Max of attention. When friends visited, they were told not to fuss over the infant, but to play with Max. He began to help feed the baby, and he showed an all-around brotherly sense of responsibility toward his sister, which he continued into adolescence."

She pounded the floor with her stick trying to get her son's attention. "But from a robust, delightful child, he became a sad, angry boy with a food problem. I recall constant feeding problems and, I'm sorry to say, I didn't handle the situation as intelligently as I should have.

"Max's development had progressed normally, and he made friends on the street. That is, until his father moved back to the city with his new wife. Max visited them on the weekends. When he returned home on Sunday from those visits, he would vomit. This vomiting continued for one month until I couldn't stand it any longer. I screamed at him, I scared him: 'If you do that once more, I'll make you clean it up, you bad boy.' The vomiting stopped. Around that time, his father disappeared for over four years.

"I had no money and an only occasional singing job, so the two kids and I moved in with my parents. But there were terrible scenes. I tried to generate their respect for their father, but it was impossible. Yet, in many ways, Max's development seemed perfectly normal. His grades were good, he had many friends, and he went into activities and sports. But he was always extremely stubborn and sensitive. He had rituals, too. For example, before going to bed, he would pull down all the window shades. A small thing, I know, but it perturbed me."

She stopped her story there, assuring me she would mail me the rest. Then she turned to her son. "Max, do you want to stay here?"

Max made no reply. His mother pounded the floor again. "Well, damn it, you will stay with these nice people. They can help you."

Max had brought no clothes with him, though his mother said he had an extensive wardrobe. I phoned his assigned houseparents, who came to the office to escort him to the cottage. As he left, I noticed he clutched in his hand a crumpled piece of paper, an old wipe, napkin, or newspaper, which he used as an intercedent between his hand and anything he touched.

Max moved into the unit but refused to interact with anyone, neither patients nor houseparents. During family group sessions he sat on his haunches or stood in a dark corner, peering out at everyone with a superior stare. Too intelligent for mere human emotion? I wondered.

The close family living conditions, with both houseparents always present, provided Max with a powerful and supportive structure. Signs of his inner warmth began to show: color in his face, a limber to his body movements. And as the air around him began to lighten, I discarded my earlier suspicion of brain damage.

After forty-six days on the unit, he tried to join in discussions, listening to others and punctuating his own words with a polite, animated half-grin. But something seemed to be missing. I believed he was more directed by mind and will than by inner feelings. There could be a command center in his brain ordering his every reaction.

Max was always on time for meals, but he would sit in the same unobtrusive corner of the long table. The housemother filled his plate first, to ensure that he got his share. He had no sense of competition with one housemate, a huge man and a massive eater, who must have appeared to Max as though he might devour him, should the food supply run out (which, of course, was never the case).

Max's ate with peculiar rituals. He clenched his utensils with two fingers in a clawlike grip. He chopped his food with a spoon into the smallest bite-size pieces. He placed peas one by one on his knife and rolled them into his mouth. And he chewed in motion so slow, the movement of his Adam's apple could barely be seen. Meat he never touched; vegetables and sweet desserts were his preferences. It was clear why his weight remained constant—between 106 and 110 pounds. For Max, eating was a painful experience.

Mrs. Cowen had shipped Max's wardrobe, but it hung in the closet untouched, just as it had in her home. His assortment of business suits, at least five years out of style, were in drab shades of gray, dark green, and brown.

One day a family assistant took a dark gray suit from Max's closet. When Max saw her hold it up to the light, he reacted with abject terror, as though her life was in immediate danger. Did he consider the suit a dangerous substance that would contaminate anyone who touched it?

As spring came to the countryside, Max exchanged his burlap for a white tee shirt and added dark, drab, oversized gabardines which he gathered twice around his bone-thin frame with a black belt. He wore old black shoes without socks and never wore underwear.

Over time, Max's teeth had yellowed to the color of old ivory and were as crusted as his hair, while his toothbrush remained as clean as a new bone. Only with the firm and constant pressure of the entire unit family would he condescend to take showers, and then only when they marched him into the bathroom, removed his clothes, lifted him to the warm spray, and scrubbed him down.

Max never slept in bed. For much of the night he stood in one position, gesturing in the dark and moving his lips as if in prayer. At daybreak he basked shirtless in the sun's rays, stroking his arms, chest, face, and head as though bathing under a crisp, clear waterfall. He always carried what looked like an old napkin, and when asked why he carried it he would retort, "Why do you ask?" Thus he parodied the psychoanalytic process; he, the analyst, was putting the patient, the asker of the question, on the defensive. He had polished this warding-off technique so well that even the most experienced professional faltered in further conversation.

Max received letters from his mother, his friends, and his former classmates, most of whom were practicing physicians. All of the letters remained unopened, stacked neatly on his dresser. He neither wrote nor called anyone.

During his third month of treatment, two psychiatrist friends wanted to visit him. When I asked him if he wanted to see them, he remained stubbornly silent. Nevertheless I extended an invitation, hoping for some emotional exchange. When they arrived, Max stood in a corner, as though engaged in prayer, and refused to talk to them.

Outside, I asked them if they had come voluntarily. I felt sure Max believed his mother had persuaded them to visit.

"Yes, his mother did call us," one of the visitors replied, "but we wanted to see him. He's a good guy but he's been this way a long time. He does look a bit more relaxed, though. We'll be back. Don't give up."

A month later, a glowingly intense student from the community college volunteered to work with Max. He tried to bury her with all his old tricks in the hope she would quit. Her answer to his airborne karate chops was, "Come here, little boy, put your head on my lap."

She would hold him, rock him, tickle him under the rib cage. Some of Max's rigidity would melt to the point where he might attempt a weak smile. By the fourth day of tickling, the rigidity had almost withered away. He hollered,

"Stop, please stop!" She retaliated with, "Okay, I'll stop if you drink a warm bottle." He capitulated, wanting no more tickling. After drinking the eight ounces of warm, sweet milk, he slept for two hours.

But the next day wasn't so successful. For ten minutes he pushed the nipple to and fro against his cheek. Finally the bottle landed on the floor. On his hands and knees, Max reached for the bottle, only to throw it across the room. "That nipple is dirty and contaminated!" he shouted, assuming a menacing and threatening posture. "Someone is trying to poison me!" The bewildered student, awed by Max's ability to bring out buried feelings of her own ineptitude (she wasn't experienced in giving adults nurturing bottles), was rendered helpless.

His obsession with contamination flew in the face of fact. In the cottages, houseparents insist that patients participate in household chores, with activity centered around the kitchen, the hearth of the home. Patients take out trash, vacuum carpets, wash floors, clean bathrooms, cook, and wash and dry dishes. The patients are responsible for making their beds and keeping private living space habitable.

Max refused every chore except washing and drying the dishes. He fumbled with the soap and water and held the washcloth with his fingernails so that no part of his skin would touch the dishes. As for drying, after ten hours on the drainboard the dishes dried themselves.

Five months passed; Max had progressed no further and had even lost some early gains. His initial interest in sharing in community life and friendship had waned. He had become unpopular with other patients, spurning them with unwarranted contempt and disdain, forcing them to see him as freakish.

After Max met every gesture of warmth with a brick wall and attempts at physical contact with angry outbursts, a former patient who was a volunteer suggested collective tickle therapy. Since this woman had firsthand experience with similar pathos both in herself and in her family, her suggestion seemed workable, even though a few considered it outlandish.

So, during one session, everybody present lifted

Max horizontally into the air, held him, and rocked him slowly. The height generated fear in Max, and when the former patient lifted Max's tee shirt and kissed his bare chest, he pushed her away.

"Hold his legs and extend his arms over his head," the former patient advised, tickling first his armpits, then his chest and stomach. Several others kissed his neck and forehead, and blew into his ears.

He squirmed and squealed but everyone held firmly, hoping for at least a smile. When this didn't happen after a few minutes, the experiment was discontinued. By morning, an ordinary man who had gone through all that exercise would have had the appetite of a lumberjack, but Max ate nothing. In fact, he exhibited even more withdrawal.

Two weeks passed with no change. His mother called, hoping as always for good news. When I took the call, I wondered what I could say to this woman.

I decided to start with the positive. "I'm convinced his condition isn't neurological," I responded to her anxious inquiries, "because there was initial improvement. But simple requests go unanswered. He has to be forced to eat, to shower, to brush his teeth. His hostility is overwhelming. He believes he's fighting for his life. The guy is very afraid of becoming alive."

"Oh my God," his mother cried, "it sounds like every other hospital he's ever been in. Maybe better for a time, then he digs in like a groundhog in a hole. I don't know where to go or what to do anymore."

"But it's too soon to give up," I replied.

With such strong resistance, it was useless, even unwise, to try to move ahead. Anyway, the staff needed to disengage, to find a space away from Maxwell's morbidity. During that down time, I treated other patients though always observing Max's reactions. At one point I gathered all the reports and medical records from his previous hospitalizations, and reviewed the psychological testing results and the voluminous notes written by houseparents and family assistants.

One morning I phoned Mrs. Cowen. "Is there any material around the house or in his office that might shed some light? I've got to have more information."

She called me several days later. "Dr. Honig, I

found some letters buried in his coat pockets, and a diary that goes way back. I believe this diary was written before he became sick, about the time he withdrew from work."

She promised to forward everything to me. Meanwhile, there were more hospital records to review. Max was indeed a strange bird. He had many of the characteristics of the *musselmanner,* the walking dead of the Nazi death camps, those who did not fight back but fatalistically surrendered to become living corpses. Bettelheim described these people as being so deprived of self-esteem and stimulation, so totally exhausted both physically and emotionally, that they surrendered to the environment.

Max appeared to be without feeling, mechanical, robotlike— a shell of a person who fought anyone carrying warmth. Such people are often seen on the back wards of large institutions. Some, like Max, are quiet, while others scream constantly, presenting a disturbing mixture of cacophony and melody that serves only the insanity and leaves its victim tortured and terrorized. Slavelike and welcoming death, these people dare not remember what freedom was, nor even dream of its return.

There was another side to Maxwell, however. He would appear quiet and alone. With sunken chest and bowed head, he had knuckled under, but to whom? And why? He had an extensive inner system that he answered to, but he had traveled both sides of the border, doctor and patient. Wise to verbal intrusion, he had mastered and defied all the therapeutic ploys and tools of the trade. But there was explosive anger deep inside him.

I was faced with a three-pronged dilemma: a patient who was not responding; managed care only too eager to label the treatment custodial so they could discontinue payment; and a fearful mother ready to throw me on the garbage mound of ineptitude, as she had done with the rest of the medical profession.

At home one evening, reviewing the report from the psychiatric hospital, I read, "Mother away on many trips during his infancy (traveling with opera productions throughout the country); father cared for him at home."

One day Max had revealed to the treating doctor that

he distrusted women. "I resent them," he said. "They take the man away. They resent me being with a man."

Maxwell demanded that people come to him rather than his going to them, according to the report. What about that awful omnipotence? I wondered. Max often repeated, "I don't have any problems, only issues of concern." I'd seen this omnipotence before, always thinking it had come from parents and been perpetuated by others, who overpraise a child, saying he's better than other children and praising him or her unrealistically for actions that the child knows he or she has not earned. The child feels inadequate; the parents sense inadequacy, deny it, and turn it into the opposite, which confuses the child. He or she may then end up with a false sense of superiority.

His father had married and divorced four times. Rather excessive! How did this affect the boy, I wondered.

For his last hospitalization, a court-ordered involuntary commitment had been needed. Yet now he never mentioned leaving The Clinic.

He had isolated himself in his apartment, studying supernatural subjects. Doctors thought he had a tremendous fear of abandonment, with immense internal rage. Had his mother failed to provide that protective shield from excessive stimuli by her frequent absences during that vulnerable first nine months of life? Was this the clue to Max's refusal to eat meat? Did his quasi-veggie diet keep him weak and passive as a shield against the tremendous internal rage?

The hospital report concluded, "Despite apparent progress in the therapeutic relationship, this patient refuses to change."

Our psychologists had tested Max within a month of his arrival. The issuing report deemed that Max was "well defended against intrusion, evoked transference rescue fantasies with his passive seduction, used magic to further his isolation from people." The doctors had concluded that he "showed long-term memory loss, had a closed and cautious profile, with a well-entrenched personality."

I wondered whether he had a secret, hidden religion, and whether the praying and the dawn and dusk sun worship might be manifestations of that religion.

I reread the six-month hospital summary: Max's

first six months were marked by the development of a relationship with his therapist characterized by mutual feelings of involvement. However, he exhibited an intense resistance to openness and a lack of apparent movement.

At the hospital, both therapist and nursing staff had grown to accept the idea that they had to tell him what to do. He became more compliant, although he remained unchanged internally. For example, simple controls worked. Extra feedings of snacks and supplements such as Sustacal brought his weight up from a low of 104 pounds to 120 or 125 pounds. Also, a prescribed schedule of personal hygiene was initiated.

A new series in treatment was begun on all fronts. Medication (the antipsychotics) were vastly increased. A dermatologist provided topical creams for his red and scaly feet and scalp. Reluctantly, he agreed to trim both finger and toe nails. Supervised visits began with his mother. Work in therapy or permanent hospitalization were the choices, i.e., *Damn it, change your strange ways. Progress!*

Max then started to discuss his "resistance," and talked of inner experiences. These included anxiety about being under another's control because of fear of the consequences; frustration because he was made to face "unpleasantness" while preferring to do what he wanted to do, when he wanted to do it; the feeling that, while he saw he had problems and needs, there was no point in facing them, since he couldn't be helped; and, most confusing, a need to preserve pride and self-respect by refusing to cooperate, even though cooperation might mean more freedom. A desperate clinging to his image as a last bastion of ego identity became a crucial issue in the treatment.

The hospital therapist concluded: "Despite some apparent progress, mostly in his relationship with me and some areas of daily life, the patient's psychosis has not fundamentally been altered. I see no change in his 'system' of delusional beliefs, including fears of contamination from people or inanimates. His passive compliance with ward management, his lack of initiative even to bathing and changing clothes, is an enormous physical and emotional drain on nursing staff. Failure to progress toward more responsibility for his own care is a poor prognostic indicator, and threatens to make it impossible to retain him on this service."

2. Discovery

The written releases and the psychiatrist's summary from the New York hospital fell short of relevant information, so I went back to Mrs. Cowen's biography.

I read that Max was five when his sister was born and that his father left soon afterwards. Each time Max visited his father, he would vomit on returning home. From being a robust, healthy youngster, he became a sad, angry, and stubborn child. He was afraid to show any anger toward his father, for fear that his father would withdraw what little love he still offered Max.

Max began seeing an analyst, Dr. Amos Mosher, who was also the professor he worshiped as a guru. But, Mrs. Cowen wrote, "I distrusted Mosher and believed him to be a spiritual con. I also believed that nothing good would come from the relationship."

One night she found written notes that Max had made, which she called the "Mosher Papers." Addressed to "Dear Ami," they confirmed her doubts. Max was twenty-six at the time.

"Oh, Ami," Max wrote, "it's happening again. God, it's hard to get up in the morning. Outside is a thick, full rain. I want to flow as freely. There are fantasies in me aching to come out. God, I envy the rain. The more I look at it, the more it hurts. It is like the world. The more I really look at it, the more I let myself feel it, the more it hurts when I can't live with it, touch it, get myself up to it, destroy it, rebuild it. I wonder if that is why I like the rain, so I can feel at least a possibility of freedom. If it turned out that each drop of rain was screaming in terror and pain as it raced toward the ground, I would probably nod and understand. Yet I know this is just an obsession. The rain flows, it does not cry. Please, God, it does not cry. How once I felt pure."

I was already aware that Max had a passion to protect all living things. "The creatures and the plants weren't meant to be destroyed," he would say. In spring, when we planted the vegetable and flower gardens, he insisted on planting his own garden, made up of newly picked and discarded weeds which he had tenderly gathered.

As I went on reading, I was amazed to discover that Max had been going under, losing it, long before anyone had realized. "God, how once I felt pure," he'd written, "How once I prayed. Once I was so frightened, and wanted to feel safe, an ally stronger and more benevolent than all others. It must have been a Mother-God, because I did not want it to demand."

He wrote about the sun and its overwhelming explosive power, how he hated hot sunny days, how they moved him to a point of explosion and noncontrol. He wrote that the sun was "a driving rapist, relentless, persistent until the world bursts into pieces or has a release. The rain, the earth, the woman finally yielding her loins and flowing."

There were notes of his struggle with death and personal disintegration. Nietzsche, Swedenborg, Clifford Beers, and others had written about similar personal experiences: the dread that accompanies the entry into insanity.

He wrote: "Two possibilities seem clear. One, annihilation, but there is something positive about annihilation, that the covering of something is torn off, and there are just molecules of free experience, a world of untamed events. I want the path to the soul and into the soul to be nice and soft and unpainful."

As I read, I realized that Max was frightened of love. He seemed confused about his identity. Man? Woman? Androgynous? And with passivity, he demanded to be pursued, to be won over in love. I read on: "Oh, God, how different my day would be if this morning I had been dragged from my bed to the bamboo poles, or even tied to the bedpost and whipped and whipped.

"Or whipped into screaming unconsciousness, fucked, and left there to sleep. This morning, I awoke nervous, wanting, horny. I felt the empty space that was filled just the time before. The air was hot but I could feel a sense of cold where the warm skin had drawn away. A woman who had been lying with the full weight of her head and chest against my abdomen suddenly rose, and I had that sense of a part of my body ripping away with a giving birth, like a sensation. And then the feeling of being alone again.

"I thought of Mosher and others getting married to resolve the madness of all the pretty women on the streets. All the possibilities and all the madness. Writing, writing to put the anxiety into some clothes so it wouldn't be so bare, so raw and hurting. Writing to be familiar, to cope with the day, the day that does not have to start with being whipped and fucked. Suppression, inhibition. Thinking about that job offer to work with the fourteen people from the drug program. Thinking about breaking them up into smaller groups of seven, a woman or two in each. The women needing to be scourged, whipped, and fucked by the male members of the group. (You don't do that in small groups, as a therapist. You don't do that when people come to you, expecting to see a rational, stable, mature therapist.) If they really want broken bargains, might not this be a superb way to begin!...Is this just a manifestation of my craziness, my neurosis, my inhibitions, my unableness)."

I tried to make sense of the stream-of-consciousness writing that depicted thoughts of love, sex, punishment, torture. This now very dead human being had once been magnificently alive. Or was it all fantasy existing only in his writings?

I continued to read: "I thought this morning of lobsters, how they are killed and opened for cooking, and I thought of it happening to people quickly and efficiency. I think it was happening to a woman, a full-body-type woman. Her body was grabbed up at one time, laid down on a table, a big, shiny knife brought swiftly down, plunged in a loud withering loop into her head, silent screams. Torn right down the middle, cracked open into two halves (still connected at the back). One large hand holding while another reaches in and indifferently pulls out the lines of organs, the nerves running up the back. Crack! a long blade crashes down the arm and it is open. Crack! the blade descends again. The leg is severed wide. Crack! the knee is open to make passage to the meat more easily. Crack!

Crack! The machine that works in the fresh-people store lifts a fresh person, runs her under the water, holds a hand over the front so none of the meat falls out, shakes off the excess water, plops her down neatly in the center, tucks in the stringy pieces of arms and legs hanging over the side, tears off a piece of wrapping paper, wraps a string around it...$4.48, please. Thank you. Good bye."

In everyday existence, this guy never eats! A vegetarian. Wow! His fantasies are pure cannibalism! Speculating on the inner workings of his unconscious, I would see a deep fear of eating and a deeper fear of retaliation, the talionic principle: eat, and be yourself eaten. So complete a deprivation of all pleasure he has! No serpent will tempt this fellow to eat a sweet apple.

Then I read: "If I am raped, then I am not guilty. I didn't want it. It is not my hunger. It is not me that wants to suck, or fuck, or kill, or fill, or love. Being bound and gagged so that nothing will get out. A mask placed around my head so that nothing could be seen, smelled, heard. There would be no feedback to my whimper. He or she would stop when the blood flowed or the twitching stopped, or until there was no more flesh, no more body life—not until the whipping in them was finished. And I wouldn't know when that would be. There would be no control, no way of handling or controlling. I might die."

I reread this paragraph, looking for a way to reach Max. I remembered the religious practices of the medieval flagellants who scourged themselves in public penance before God.

There must be a way, I read on, to get the mind and body to dance, to hear the music and flow with it.

"Liar, fraud," I read, "you know you'd be scared of that....We are all women to our souls. The soul is God. Yet just think—if he could make you not need to run, how beautiful that would be."

Putting aside the massive pile of papers, I took a deep breath. What did it all mean? Where is the clue to Maxwell's emotional prison? He wrote of a wish to be reunited with his father. Of course, that was in his other life, when he was still going to work every day. Maybe this was the hoped-for realization of the childhood dream. His father

125

had left at such an early, critical time in his life. He still craved his father's love, even though he was an adult, and he probably blamed his mother for what happened then, just as many children do. This diary clearly showed his identity confusion.

Did he write of hope or its opposite? Was Maxwell signaling that he was too weak to try again? And that he was so entrenched in his miserable existence that nothing would change it?

What did those fantasies of rape and torture mean? And what to do with someone so guarded? What were the choices? If I said he was untreatable, wouldn't this be playing God? Should I proceed, looking at his discomfort and his inability to help himself, to break into his defenses like a breaker ship in an ocean of ice, and lift him from the frigid sea?

It was a difficult decision, especially since he continued to resist. There are those people who would defend his right to resist, and the law is not clear as to what intrusion might be allowed or not allowed.

I have treated the children and husbands and wives of psychiatrists, social workers, psychologists, and even the professionals themselves—all kinds of people for whom the words and phrases that express emotion, such as *trust me with your life* and *personal gratification* and *you are a beautiful person,* have lost their magic in dysfunction. They have fallen into a prostitution of intimacy, because they have lost their honesty and trust.

Was this the case in Maxwell's early years? He had convinced himself and at least one other (an adolescent housemate believed he had potent powers of magic) that his was the only way, and that everyone else was crazy. He had said he wasn't crazy, but simply going through a "change in life style." He had become a master of cooling down emotions whenever an aura of high intensity began to charge the air. And another thing! What were these strange quasi-religious rituals that he performed? He was the High Priest, a guru, the only person giving wise and authoritative decisions and opinions. But where were his followers?

3. Without Identity

I refused to accept the possibility that despite the intensity and thoroughness of my search for information, along with hours of personal involvement, I still did not know Maxwell Cowen, M.D. To accept that would be tantamount to failure.

I did have to admit, however, that he was a shell of what he once had been, an automaton following the commands of a phantasm that moved either around him or within him. He had given up. The shards of his past life now lived only in his mother's hopes, and in the faces of two friends from college. Only when I looked into their eyes did I knew that Max had, indeed, once lived.

Late into the night, I read Max's letters to Dr. Amos Mosher, trying to feel what Max had been. I believed that it was that ethereal being I had to contact, then merge with. I had to recreate him within myself, to take all I knew of his inorganic carcass and conjure up a spirit from what others said about him.

How? I could imagine myself the woodcarver, carving an image of dried mahogany. Like Giuseppe, I would carve a Pinocchio and, when I finished, this being would lie lifeless until I breathed life into him. My triumph would be the recreation of a human being, a colleague, a fellow physician set free to be a happier warrior against life's miseries.

As his physician, I could not let him rot, nor could I "give advice which may cause his death"; if our roles had been reversed, I would have wanted Maxwell, as my physician, to do everything in his power to heal me.

I thought back to what maybe had happened.

Maxwell Cowen, M.D., had been known as a gifted young psychiatrist, loved by colleagues and fellow workers and in demand for his skills in treating patients. He had been a candidate in psychoanalysis. Treating a teacher of the same age as himself who believed he had active tuberculosis, Max, as is proper in a professional relationship, jumped in with all his energy, as I might have done, as I was doing now, waxing enthusiasm and confidence, overflowing with the healing arts, wishing to minister, revive, cure.

The doctor-healer assimilates, holds, recreates within himself or herself what the patient feels without losing his or her own boundaries. Absorbing the patient's misery allows the weaker of the two to remain vulnerable and absorb the strength of the stronger. Thus a transfusion of the spirit takes place. In the end, the doctor will become depleted and exhausted, but with rest he or she soon is rejuvenated. It seemed Dr. Cowen had lacked the strength to rejuvenate himself. Not only did his patient fail to recover but he, the doctor, succumbed.

Now, after five years, Max found it impossible to acknowledge this failure. In place of any memory stood a bizarre and mystical religion replete with ritual and purification that directed his daily activity. And his will surrounded this purulence like the shell of the tortoise, a barricade against all intrusion.

This mysterious quasi religion was a rationalization, a justification of the only position he could take. It gave form and voice, however distorted, to whatever human feeling remained within him. In Max's case, it was the only alternative to suicide. In order to survive in an overwhelming world, he had retreated to an isolated microcosm of which he was, himself, the involuntary Creator; others could not enter this bubble of existence, nor could he escape. Endangered by forces he could neither control nor collaborate with, he surrendered to the safety of a prison cell.

But these elaborate and bizarre mechanizations for either shutting out the world or shutting himself in could never succeed. Never was he at ease, but always tense, distrustful, afraid. Never did he sleep. Instead, he remained eternally vigilant outside his own prison. But who was the oppressor?

Perhaps there had been a measure of inhumanity in some of his treatments. He did not want medication, but the courts forced drug treatment on him. And when small amounts had no effect, larger and larger doses were prescribed. Even the most recently discovered antipsychotic medications that in others had produced miraculous changes in mood, worked against Max.

He had been a patient on a psychiatric ward of a general hospital, a hospital full of operating rooms, cardiac monitors and supplies of oxygen, a hospital where babies were being born. This life-sustaining, life-giving environment may seem to be the essence of hope, but not to its inhabitants. Research shows no one can live comfortably for more than thirty days in a general hospital without undergoing decompensating effects on the psyche. Locked doors, sterile instruments, restrictive repression of emotion—all spanking clean, and all deeply inhumane.

I now believed that Max had been brainwashed, not by external forces but from within. A prisoner whose spirit accepts defeat will obey whatever orders are given—to eat, to sleep, to march into a death chamber—and it makes little difference if he questions or resists because his fate is already sealed.

I also believed that, in the beginning, Max had an acute psychotic breakdown, a distortion of consciousness, a psychophysiologic reaction resulting in an open wound that never healed.

The process of "going crazy" is comparable to falling asleep, as first described by Otto Isakower. As the sane person goes through the twilight zone between consciousness and sleep, he or she feels the world slipping away. This person senses a moment of anxiety before the loss of consciousness. Then comes a feeling of floating, or disembodiment, followed by sleep.

But in psychosis the anxiety builds into feelings of dread. Dread gives way not to sleep but to feelings of impending doom, of world-ending catastrophe. At this point, suicide may occur. Says the individual: *I will preempt my imminent death by controlling how and when it will happen.* But what happens most often is a lapse into insanity.

Max had never recovered from the acute psychosis. He did not kill himself. Instead, he drifted into a worsening state and entered the ranks of the chronically mentally ill.

I refused to believe that it was too late for him. I had a few ideas, but all were fraught with danger. The land-grant state hospital system was first established, over one hundred years ago, as a protection for the mentally ill. But abuses had awakened the argument between the Constitutional Bill of Rights, a banner lifted high by the legal profession, and the right to treatment with a chance for recovery, a concern of the medical profession. Written regulations protected both rights, but, filled with procedural requirements and treatment restrictions, they left little room for exploration or interpolation.

I was aware that the methods of therapy I was considering were unconventional and would challenge the legal interpretation of the regulations. These regulations speak of a treatment plan signed by the patient (written informed consent). Max never touched a pen, neither to sign anything nor to write a letter. Physical restraints were allowed only to prevent danger to the patient or others, unlike chemical restraints (drugs) that are accepted as part of therapy. And I needed to consider the Federal Regulations on the Protection of Human Subjects that outline strict rules for experimentation on human beings, for some would consider the proposed treatment experimental.

I needed support from my colleagues. I would begin with the professional staff, a polyglot batch with beliefs that ranged from *mental illness is a nonexistent myth* to *it is all either biologic or genetic in origin*. I hoped that most of them would listen to reason and allow me to present my case. The worst nightmare would be an unending bureaucratic entanglement that might forever hold up procedures especially designed for Max.

With this in mind, I asked the medical and clinical staff to meet with me as soon as possible.

4. The Meeting

I began the meeting by stating that the first thirty days of any case, this case in particular, were often a physician's dream. I invited the assembled social workers, nurses, psychologists, physicians, and nonprofessionals to interrupt any time they had comments or questions.

Max had settled in at The Clinic and frequently said this was his first real home ever and his houseparents were the best mother and father he'd ever known. Platitudes though these words might be, his true feelings came out in his actions, such as the way he found little ways to help around the home. We've learned to be cautious, so we often refer to this phenomenon as the honeymoon—a time when patients get acquainted with the entire place and most are on their best behavior.

Little by little, the honeymoon glow is fated to vanish, as it did in Max's case. He did try to stay near others, especially in the evening. But lack of appetite brought on fear of impending doom, followed by a sense of immobilization. Statue posturing, edematous ankles, back bent like a horseshoe, wrinkled face, disappearing smile: there was no way to stop this downward spiraling.

His sparkle-deserted eyes began to sink as though in quicksand. Unwashed clothes rotted on his frame, his shoes were never strung, his hair matted, his beard lengthened, his skin flaked and decayed, and he always held a crushed napkin in his hand.

In the beginning he was angry at his own weakness but, with ever-increasing mental pain, he had no escape but to turn inward. It had worked before. He had become an untouchable, a mystical blue god of the glacier age, a zombie, a living corpse. The insanity had become too powerful for his will alone to fight.

At the meeting I summarized the many treatments we had attempted. At first we had emphasized positive reinforcement: nurturing, massage, warm baths, bedtime stories, music (he had tried to extend his clawlike fingers on the guitar). As things turned sour, the staff tried all kinds of verbal confrontation; these included directly interpreting his behavior and assailing all of his senses, sounds, looks, and smells.

I had flown at Max's inability to take nourishment, associating this with his lack of maternal and paternal attention during childhood growth phases. I had born down on his failure in sibling rivalry, his parents' divorce, his wanting his father yet hating him at the same time. Still the depression and regression had deepened. He had touched not a crayon in art; no rhythm had come from his rigid body in dance therapy. Tickling and holding him were tantamount to touching rigor mortis. All the while, insurance companies were becoming impatient and family savings were diminishing.

"What do you make of this case?" asked a social worker.

"Suppose he gave up his psychosis as a snake sheds a skin to make room for further growth. What would he be?" came from a psychiatrist.

"Wouldn't it be wonderful if he became the doctor, the healer he once was." I was riding a magic carpet, not facing the fact that Max was emotionally depleted.

"There is little doubt in my mind that Max has been brainwashed," I told the group. "I admit I had thought he might have had a brain tumor or diabetes, because of his repetitive mouth movements, his slow mentality, his emaciation. But with the surge of improvement over the past three months, it all reversed. In retrospect, these symptoms were caused by emotional and physical depletion with disuse of his frontal lobes."

I explained the theory of brainwashing, as seen in the techniques used in Russia, China, and Vietnam to elicit confessions and induce sudden political conversions, as well as in Nazi Germany. Cults and terrorists also use such methods. It's all a perversion of Pavlov's work. These techniques of breaking down the spirit include sleep deprivation, humiliation, intimidation, the big lie, threats to family members, loud noises, bright light, false expectations, death threats, directives to stand in one position, food and fluid deprivation, squalor, and isolation.

These techniques are not dissimilar to the cunning and imaginative modus operandi of command hallucinations. Rewards and periods of relative quiescence foster dependency on interrogators. In psychosis, dependency is encouraged by higher hallucinations that speak as friends. The patient is sucked in by these friendly hallucinations, and exit becomes difficult. Ultimately he or she becomes trapped by the negative voices of self-denigration.

Why are some people able to resist brainwashing?

Masud Khan suggested the term *cumulative trauma* to describe a lifetime of startling psychophysical experiences that have a lasting effect on mental life.

Anna Freud wrote, "subtle harm is being inflicted on the child, the consequences of it will become manifest at some future date." Those so injured, beginning early, remain in need of adoration and protection continually. It is these people that are easily brainwashed. It is also this population that remains vulnerable to psychosis and other emotional illnesses. Fortunately, most people have cumulative life experiences that do not leave them easily vulnerable to psychosis.

Like many before him, Max had tried to find the cause and the reason for his suffering. He did this through his letters to Ami. All pain transgresses the body, enters the mind, and turns to the ethereal soul for answers.

Emmanuel Swedenborg, a physician and later the founder of the Swedenborgian faith, wrote in 1747: "...evil spirits are such they regard man with deadly hatred, and desire nothing more than to destroy him, body and soul."

Swedenborg wrote of possession by evil spirits as patients speak of hallucinations: "When spirits enter consciousness, they speak in man's native tongue, they seek to destroy his conscience, and are against every higher value. They suggest acts against the person's conscience and, if refused, threaten, and make them seem more plausible, or do anything to overcome the person's resistance—lie, seduce, deceive."

In my presentation, I determined that Maxwell was indeed a complicated individual. To believe he had simply been brainwashed, and that consequently undergoing a deprogramming would return him to sanity, seemed naive. If so, I could ignore the writings to Ami. Yet I could not ignore the signs of mind control— the dogmatism, robot repetitiveness, poor nutrition, and personal degradation—all of which occur with brainwashing.

However, Maxwell showed little sign of being an obedient follower of any charismatic leader. Nor did he evince idealism or hard work for any group or cause. I began to believe that, like Swedenborg, Maxwell displayed elements of demonic possession.

Charles Wesley had been an ineffectual preacher to the respectable in early-eighteenth-century London. He believed that spiritual salvation could be achieved by the performance of good works, and not by faith alone. He suffered a severe mental breakdown and sought out Peter Bohler, a Moravian minister, and went through a

133

conversion. He soon influenced his more talented preacher brother, John, to undergo a similar conversion. John Wesley hit upon an extremely important technique of conversion. He learned to create high emotional tension in his audience by preaching that the failure to achieve salvation would be condemnation to Hellfire. Wrote a disciple:

> He would stroke back his hair, turn his face toward me, place his eyes upon me. His countenance struck such an awful dread even before I heard him speak that it made my heart beat like the pendulum of a clock. And when he spoke, I felt it all directed at me.
>
> Immediately, one and another and another [of the audience] sunk to the earth. They dropped on every side as thunderstruck....Wesley heightened the excitement with static electricity, using a Leyden jar to collect the charge. A shock to the convert's body enhanced the ecstasy.

I continued: "It is unlikely, says William Sargant, that Billy Graham will have the same success as Wesley, not only because he doesn't have the support of follow-up systems but also because he avoids the mention of Hell. To be successful in conversion, both extremes of life and death, or Heaven and Hell, must be felt with the fullest range of emotion, from despair to the height of ecstasy.

"Will James said that emotional occasions, especially violent ones, are extremely potent in precipitating mental arrangements. Emotions that come in this way seldom leave things as they found them.

"There are elements of both brainwashing and demoniac possession in Max's illness. De-brainwashing techniques would be too concrete, too shallow to reach the patient's soul. But the intense emotion awakened during the psychodrama of an exorcism might reach the inner depth necessary to convert him once again into a human being."

The professional staff approved of an exorcism to treat Max. They recommended that it be confined within the parameters of a psychodrama, and that inordinate quantities of nurturing be supplied all through the process.

5. *The Exorcism*

Max's daily treatment never stopped. Before, during, and after each meeting, we chiseled away at his defensive armor. After each outpouring of emotion I felt more exhausted, and I often felt overcome with pessimism.

Max seemed to sense penetration of his defenses and became verbal, using psychoanalytic jargon that he had learned in training, but as an implement to rebuff intimate association. Empty, flattering words ("I am getting better, you are helping me, what a marvelous place....The family model is the answer to all of psychiatry's problems") flowed like Niagara, misleading everyone. The odor from his room had become unbearable. Piles of feces were wrapped neatly in toilet paper like loaves of bread dough made ready for the oven.

At night he continued secret seances, but this time with an audience. A pitiful thirteen-year-old delusional boy stood in fear and awe of Maxwell, seeing in him the personification of wicked and bedeviled occult powers, hoping that power would be magically transferred to him. Max was aware of his own sinister influence and used it often to enhance his leverage over the house staff who were split as to the best approach to his condition.

The boy adored him but his ardor was not reciprocated. It was this lack of concern on Max's part that led the younger patient to reveal Max's secret. In a group session, which of course included Max, he said, "He has a magic bar of soap, only it's dry. He holds it over his head every night with both hands like a priest holding up a cross of Jesus to God."

Sensing an opportunity for an improvisational drama, I began to pace and wave my arms about, raising my voice to a higher and higher pitch as Max watched. "Well, where is this bar of soap, if it really is a bar of soap?"

"It's in my room," Max answered, "next to my toothbrush and comb. And it *is* a bar of soap."

But a search of his belongings produced neither toothbrush, toothpaste, nor a bar of soap.

"He's lying to you," said the youthful disciple, who was filled with admiration at Max's ability to deceive. "It's in his back pocket."

Max clutched the rear pockets of the suit he once wore as a practicing psychiatrist and began to shout over and over that there was nothing inside the pockets. He looked with disdain at his devotee, shouting "You are lying!" to the committed lad, the only person with faith in him.

I had an eerie feeling that this was an act before suicide which would remove the last vestige of any link between himself and the human race. Immediate action was necessary. "Take down his pants!" I shouted.

Kicking and shouting, he dug his hands into his right rear pocket. His purple fingers were pulled from the torn pants. Out of the right pocket came a flat, round object made of circular strands of woven hair, approximately the size of a small orange. Seven concentric circles of this tightly woven hair surrounded a space the size of a penny. The hair was held together by matted secretions of saliva and nasal drippings, although Max claimed it came from different regions of his head.

I held the object in the cup of my extended palms, marveling at the workmanship. It had within it the feeling of holiness, the preservation of religious ritual, the atavistic Godhead, a symbol of the struggle of life over death in primitive culture.

"Aha! A mandala," I exclaimed.

The thirteen-year-old lunged for the artifact, as though holding it would instill in him what he believed Max had, the security of being grounded to the earth.

"No, no...don't let him touch it," Max sputtered. He was as purplish as a bloodworm and surprisingly without sweat. I placed the mandala, so delicate in feature, upon a section of the morning newspaper, and continued with the session.

"What is this thing? What do you use it for?" I asked.

"It's nothing. I just did some weaving to pass the time," was his blasé answer.

Had we discovered the vital element of Max's divine might, the core of a belief system from which flowed the life blood of his realities? This was not the textbook picture of schizophrenia, the raving lunatic with hallucinations and delusions, nor of the chronic paranoid with a thinking disorder so extreme he could be mistaken for a retard.

Oh, yes, he had once lived the life of a vagrant, moving from soup kitchen to abandoned doorway, eating from garbage cans, likely to eventually to die, a pauper, from pneumonic exposure or methanol poisoning. But now he was fighting with primordial passion, an unenlightened and unknowing being, and had moved into enigmatical, recondite mysticism, a position in limbo where he might view both the soul death of insanity and the joy/pain of normal life.

"Mana, animana, moma animanamana mandala," jabbered the thirteen-year-old. He had fallen to the floor in something like a trance. If not for the soft carpet, he might have bruised or fractured his skull. His hands flailed over his head and rhythmically thumped the deck. It was hours before he became quiet.

During this ruckus and confusion, Max took it upon himself to disappear. Later we saw him outside under the porch lights performing a masque, immune to the upheaval within the cottage.

"See! See!," the adolescent gestured wildly out the window. "You took away his mandala but you didn't destroy his magic! I know it. I always knew it. He has supernatural powers. And he has mana. He will possess all your souls. He has mine now, out there. Oh, I feel horrible." Exhaustion and hysterical fear had left his young body limp. We carried him from the floor to his bed. As we did so, I held one sweaty hand tightly.

"He can't hurt you while I stay here," I said. "God has commissioned me to protect you from black magic. Don't be afraid to speak freely."

His eyes glazed over as he looked at me. "To tell you all will break the taboo, and I will die. I believed in Max and he turned against me. I did love him, but now I'm afraid of him. Please help me. I don't want to die. He's a demon witch using sorcery. He says he's a shaman, but he's arrogant and doesn't believe in God. In fact, he thinks he *is* God."

He stretched his neck to look out the window. "Look at him out there. He's crazy, carrying on like that with his moon ritual. He has his own spot, out near the big rock. It's his site. Once I saw some small bones there. He talks about human sacrifice. 'It's not going to be me, is it?' I ask. But he never answers. And there's a dead rabbit hanging from a tree near the rock."

After that, the lad quietened. At sunrise Max disappeared, but since he never left the clinic grounds, I knew he wasn't far away.

I set to thinking about what had actually transpired. Our acceptance of Max and our round-the-clock nurturing had made him mentally stronger. But his ability to control the exhausted and frightened teenager was frightening, as was his mystical consultation with the heavens. Adolf Hitler also consulted the stars and, although a gourmand, he ate no red meat, just as Max eschewed red meat as a way to control the raging violence within. The guy was still as rigid in his beliefs as on the first day I met him.

Did I really believe that Max was possessed by demons? And why an exorcism?

In the proper and technical sense, exorcism is a ceremony used by the Christian Church to expel demons when they grab power. Even today it remains an integral part of the Catholic baptismal service, a way to remove impediments to grace resulting from the effects of Original Sin and the power of Satan.

A powerful illness demands an even more powerful cure. An exorcism it would be, but an exorcism in the broadest sense. We would construct a psychodrama around the themes of good and evil in the manner of the primitive ancient rites, propitiating the good and expelling the evil spirits.

I had at my disposal a sine-wave muscle stimulator that caused muscles to contract and arouse emotions, hopefully inducing an ecstatic state (remember Wesley's Leyden jar?). Perhaps this was not a pleasant stimulus, but Cairns's work showed that the greater the stimulus, the greater the attachment. Pleasant stimuli were effective, but not enough to elicit change.

Electricity to stimulate and contract peripheral muscles is not a new concept in psychiatry. S. Weir

Mitchell used electrotherapy to stimulate muscle contractions in cases of "nervous weakness" in 1887. Pliny Earle at Friends Hospital (1841), learning from Leuret's *Traitement Morale de la Folie* in the Paris Asylum Bicetre, used many physical methods to expose and extinguish patient delusions.

I presented my plan of therapy to the medical and clinical personnel on the staff, and then to the Human Rights Patient Advocacy Committee and to the Board of Directors. Mrs. Cowen wrote a letter asking for the plan to be implemented. She would assume responsibility and sign in her son's place. The plan was explained to Max. His refusal to respond with a "yes" or "no" was accepted as oral informed consent. This technicality would later lead to a controversy so out of proportion to the situation that it obscured the simple effects of the treatment itself.

The sine-wave alternating current would be administered through an electric device called the Relaxicizer (donated by a former patient's mother), available on the open market and advertised as "the most modern and sophisticated way to lose weight." Like many fads for weight reduction, it was touted by a few and decried by many.

In a trial run, the Director of Nursing and I applied the machine to our own bodies. Pads were attached to the upper thighs, calves, buttocks, abdomen, or upper arms. A half-hour workout, with increasing charge, produced a pleasurable fatigue similar to having run a 1OK race. The maximum surge contracted the muscles with maximum effort. It would certainly blend with a psychodramatic event to equal the life-and-death mystique of a trumped-up surgical operating scene.

Dressed in pale green surgical scrubs borrowed from the neighboring general hospital, and with cap, face mask, and surgical gloves in hand, the nurse and I entered the living unit, carrying the Relaxicizer in its case. The houseparents were asked for the twenty-four-hour report of Max's condition.

Blending easily into the drama about to unfold, the housemother said, "When I asked him why he didn't give you a hug yesterday before you left, he answered, 'Why do you ask?'"

"Get the straightjacket and cuffs," I shouted.

A look of alarm crossed Max's face, the first real emotional response since his breakdown. Looking around the room, I began to talk to the others about the weather and other trivia. The tension began to mount.

"Wrap him up like a mummy," I said. "I don't want to see blood all over this room. Put some hot water on to boil, spread some clean newspaper and sheets." I had begun to roll up my sleeves.

The patient stiffened his arms, showing some mock resistance with a weak "no, no," as soft restraints were applied.

"Stand him up," I said, "and drop his smelly drawers." Down came the baggy trousers, revealing an underlife of urine-stained underpants, skinny legs, and edematous ankles.

Exercising the calm of a surgeon surveying his field of operation, I showed the nurse where to apply the moist pads: both leg calves, and the quadriceps. "I'm going to wash my hands," I said reverently, "because absolute sterility is necessary when transferring brains."

Max stared at the pulsating lights, red and yellow, that flashed in syncopated rhythm. After a moment he uttered another complete sentence. "What is that thing? I don't want that thing on me."

"What are you complaining about? For a guy who doesn't want to live, why don't you die like a man?"

"What do you mean by that? Stop! Let's talk this out. It's not too late," Max said in a cracked voice.

"Stop, everyone!" I exclaimed. "The man has asked that we talk."

One of the family assistants responded, "I think he's stalling, Doctor."

"No, no," Max said. "I'll talk. What do you want me to say?" That was followed by absolute silence. Max either could not or would not say any more.

I turned up the dials again. "Ah, you're right. He faked me out. Here it comes, so get ready."

Max's calves and thighs began to jump in magical cadence, like those of a toy soldier marching mechanically on a cuckoo clock. The rigidity in his face cracked as he trembled with anxiety. In spite of his stress, his blood pressure and pulse remained normal. Perhaps the rocklike armor that surrounded his emotions was giving way.

As the pads on his forearms were activated, his arms began to bob up and down. The motions of his arms and legs resembled a windmill.

He began to shout in rhythm, "Up legs, up arms, down legs, down arms." Union had replaced anxiety.

The staff joined in with the cadence. After about ten minutes of hand clapping, I made him an offer. "If you take a nurturing bottle, we will stop."

"I'll take a bottle from you, okay?" he said.

"You've got a deal," I answered, and turned off the machine.

That weekend Max's houseparents left for vacation. Having battled Max's illness since his arrival, with Max still showing little sign of fitting into their surrogate family, they were throughly exhausted, utterly frustrated, and burnt out.

Their replacements, a younger, newly-married couple, abounded with all kinds of energy. No sooner had they arrived when Max asked his new male houseparent to play chess. That same evening, he volunteered to wash and dry the dinner dishes. What had happened? He had seen the regular male houseparent as the father he missed early in life and he needed his respect and wanted to measure up to his expectations, and with his regular female houseparent he had been caught in an inability to develop intimacy because she was the older man's wife (both tranferences time-old and veritable). Now, with the younger replacements, he could simply be friends without fear or threat.

"It was weird as a child," he told the younger wife one night in the kitchen. "Just my mother and I. We lived with my grandfather and grandmother, and were very poor. My mother slept all day, and went to the city at night. She was an actress, you know." His face lifted a second with some semblance of pride. "Some aunts and uncles were around, but I always envied the other kids who had two parents. Some of their fathers worked all day in the oil refineries and other factories in Perth Amboy, and I thought that was neat! I don't believe my mother ever faced the truth of how weird we were."

I marveled at the sudden change, not even a full day after the switch in houseparents, and even more at the possible reasons. Did the new couple magically transform the environment, or was it the effects of the new "treatment machine"? But how could a machine popular enough to be in every family practitioner's office and on the generic market, help a patient to emerge from a mental illness that had proved refractory to the latest medications, the biomedical theory, and the best that medical science had to offer?

But why fight it? It is too easy in this profession to find a reason for everything. The treatment was working, and life was emerging in Max. Perhaps we had found the only key to the door of his unconscious. If that key opened the door, and did no harm, we could do nothing less than enter.

The sessions continued. Working with only a pigeonhole of an opening, I squeezed my energy in, fully expecting it to close over quickly at any time. But now I had a wedge. True, Maxwell's defense system continued to fell trees in the road, intentionally or not. Each tree had to be removed and the path made clear.

With the Relaxiciser as my John Wesley, I attacked the contamination bugaboo until one day Max threw out his old suits and replaced them with fresh white tee shirts, white socks, jeans, and sneakers.

He also began to shower and to wash his own clothes and bed sheets. Now, with clean outfits, he umpired the baseball games and played basketball with the Clinic gang at the junior high school.

I assailed his meager, fussy eating but stopped when he confessed that his mother's food "never seemed right." With the mesmerizing Relaxicizer, he was able to negotiate an eating pattern that included all meats, cheeses, starches, and vegetables. He joined the family at the table and, in time, gained twenty-five pounds.

But living this way was "risky," he said. He was getting stronger, angrier, more aggressive, and more vulnerable to attack from other patients whom he chased off with eerie magical movements.

"I'm on this positive crest," he said one day, but he feared it wouldn't last. He was climbing the back of the insanity, success upon success. Before, when he had battled the sickness, bad things had tended to overwhelm him and he always gave in. But it was different now. Optimism, confidence, smiles—a fool's paradise?

I pushed ahead. Max agreed to test inpatients. He had learned to do this during his psychiatric residence, when he had shown "great empathy and understanding of a patient's struggle, but [was] too verbose and rambling," said his supervisor, who was sticking out his professional neck to help Max.

Max continued to drink his urine and bag his feces. When discovered, he denied doing it, blaming his former teenage disciple.

"I have just come from visiting with God," I thundered one day, "and he finds your toilet habits disgusting and unprofessional. I can't believe you're a doctor, you're so unsanitary. Do you believe your shit doesn't stink? I'm going to hook up this machine to you and me both."

He recoiled and shouted, "No, no, I can't be attached to anyone!" Then he burst into tears, which brought a flood of staff hugs. He continued sobbing. "I feel like a small bird with two broken wings that has fallen in the middle of the turnpike. Maybe one car will stop, and another, and a guy will get out and try to move the little bird. But it's dangerous to stop. It's easier to run him down, kill him, and let the world go on." He cried openly.

A prodigious amount of staff nurturing followed. Experience has shown it is the untempered outpouring of affection and adoration that does strengthening, both mentally and physically. But first, the mountain has to be moved. Fortunately, most patients have far less rigid defense mechanisms than Max.

At home one evening, I received a call from Mrs. Cowen. I described the treatment, the Relaxicizer, the aroused emotion, and the massive staff support.

"Oh, my, aren't you afraid he might become too attached and never want to leave?" she asked.

"Mrs. Cowen, that's what it's all about. Attachment

could save your son's life. We're trying like hell to make him feel something! Don't worry about too much attachment, worry about too little. If he becomes strong enough, it will be like the apple ripening on the tree. When ready, it will simply fall away. What I mean is, he won't need us anymore."

Treatment continued day by day. In time, Max came to detest the very sight, sound, or thought of the Relaxicizer. In giving up the war, he became increasingly more human. There was no way back, for even when he tried to force a return to insanity, it wouldn't happen. I was beginning to believe he would never get sick again, that he was developing an immunity to his own illness.

Wanting more, he turned to both me and the houseparents for direction. He felt he needed his own space, so he helped to transform the unit's basement into a makeshift apartment.

One morning I found him sitting in this newly created two-room suite on an orange crate covered over with a towel. He sat there looking at two wide boards, supported by cement blocks that held a large piece of thin foam rubber, his bed. In his hand was a set of papers. He threw the papers at Squeaky, his underfed alley cat that had been sleeping peacefully against a thick piece of foam, Max's pillow. After the papers floated to the ground, he bent down and retrieved the bundle, attempting to restore order.

"How am I going to do it all?" he asked as he studied the paper stack. "Assistant in general maintenance and supervision of work crew, develop and initiate other projects."

He looked around at the bare spaces. "I'm supposed to make my own furniture." He flipped another paper. "Develop inservice training for family assistants and houseparents. Develop a research program, gather data to study treatment results over the last five years, prepare medical audits, do psychological testing of inpatients, counsel outpatients."

His stipend for this work had been set at room and board and $300 a month. Clearly, he felt he'd bitten off more than he could chew.

But it was to his work as a family assistant that he directed most of his energy. With the same passion with which he had fought the machine, he fought for a place in the sun—recognition from those who not too long ago shared with him the role of patient.

But never a hero in your own backyard. Led by the young boy who had been his disciple, his patients rebelled, rebuking his authority. They went to the houseparents with complaints.

"What is a family assistant's job?" they asked. "This guy is spooky. He stands all night, stares at us, and never talks."

In a private session, Max said, "I crave being a leader of men. But it is difficult to even follow myself from one minute to the next."

But he held his ground and in time the patients turned their distemper elsewhere. Eventually he became bored with working the graveyard shift, from eleven at night to seven in the morning, where he never had to confront anyone, and he applied for day work.

"I'm tired of playing the weirdo, the ghoul. I want to be part of the life of the day," he said in session. "But I don't seem to have the energy I had before I went bananas."

I remained steadfast. "I have a court appearance with a very important case in the next county. I've been subpoenaed as an expert witness. I want you to go with me as an advisor. But you have to wear a suit."

Max hesitated.

"So, what's your answer?"

It took him five hours, but he agreed to accompany me.

The trip in the client's private limousine gave us an opportunity to talk as professionals. And the courtroom awakened in him a desire for more excursions.

"I even imagine myself a doctor again," he said later, touching the new tan gabardine suit he had purchased for the occasion. "But I have a need to please everybody. If I join one group, I'm afraid another group won't like me. I can't take a definite position on anything. Any confidence that's been built up is destroyed. The pain comes like waves of bullets through me. I feel afterwards like Swiss cheese, full of holes, completely weakened. It's difficult to begin again after each knockdown."

These times of despair alternated with times of elation and strength. He began to spend more time with a former patient, a woman who had gone through her own battle with suicide; they had lived in the same surrogate home.

He asked me where could he purchase a van. I called an auto dealer friend. Max was increasingly identifying with the working class. He wore a green mechanic's jumpsuit, even slept in it.

He enjoyed his work as a family assistant, but, in open rebellion against increased paper documentation, he never filled out coverage notes.

"If I find myself responding to programming, and get pushed too far, I get nutty. I'm beginning to see myself as handicapped," he said.

On the occasion of an hour-long conversation with Max, Mrs. Cowen was ecstatic and hugged me. "Dr. Honig, you have cured my son. I knew you could do it. I just knew it."

I nodded. "Thanks for your confidence. He is better, but he still has a long way to go."

Signs of happiness became more evident as the seasons changed. Max smiled more. He played more basketball and even became one of the softball league's most celebrated umpires, known for quick, accurate, and fair decisions. Piles of freshly laundered clothes graced a newly made clean-sheeted bed. And the trees whispered that Max was in love. He was observed in town holding hands with his woman friend. People now spoke openly for his regaining his medical license. He listened but soothed them by saying he moves best with the speed of a tortoise.

Then everything changed. A small but vocal group of professionals from The Clinic's outpatient department, unhappy with the downscaling and transfer of the entire outpatient staff to another part of the county, launched a major attack against The Clinic, claiming patient abuse.

The attack was well organized, and each recruited member was given a specific task with a different patient and their family. Their aim: destroy The Clinic and its doctors. As founder and medical director of The Clinic, as well as one of the treating doctors, I was the focus of their attack.

The group obtained access to television and newspapers, including the free supermarket pamphlets. In short order they brought charges of patient abuse to the district attorney's office, and all current patients had to undergo interviews. Since many of the accusers were part of Max's treatment team and had witnessed the use of the Relaxicizer, Max was to be the prime witness. A three-month investigation included testimony of family assistants, houseparents, and all doctors.

Eventually The Clinic was cleared of all charges, but events of that magnitude are often fraught with casualties, and this attack was no exception.

For three months I moved wherever the fires blazed. I was unable to administer the intense treatment that the patients needed. Max was no longer one of the neediest, or so I thought. As I scurried around, putting my fingers in the holes in the dike, he always seemed to be nearby, sometimes staring with baffled paralysis and sometimes offering coffee, a notepad, or a pen. He wanted to help save The Clinic but he couldn't or wouldn't talk about his own feelings.

He wore with pride a gold watch on his left wrist, and he consulted it frequently. A gift from the board of directors, it was inscribed, "To Dr. Cowen, in appreciation of service to our patients."

He watched with concern as patients returned from the courthouse after giving testimony, knowing he would soon be called. Finally two detectives arrived in a sheriff's van with a copy of the subpoena summoning him to give testimony, along with a warrant to search his apartment. But Max had disappeared. On the table in his basement apartment lay a handwritten note:

To Whom It May Concern:
I would like to express several items of concern. Not only is the career and work of Dr. Albert Honig at issue, but equally important are the lives and futures of the people he is helping, and people he has already helped.
As Director of The Clinic, he is like the head

of a family whose influence and well-being are felt as important to all those who are in his care. As head of the family, he has been providing the guidance and leadership for The Clinic, and as such, please remember that any decisions made with regard to him are going to influence the other members of his family. I think it is important, therefore, not only for Dr. Honig but for the family as a whole that he be treated in a way that would look to the welfare of all concerned.

Recently, much has been said about The Clinic. During my contact with The Clinic, I have seen and experienced many things, some of them very fine and moving, some of them less so.

There has been caring and warmth, moments of tenderness, times of antagonism or struggle. I have seen people function in a caring, patient, thoughtful manner. Other times, things moved swiftly; there were even moments when impulses seemed to get a little out of hand.

In like manner, I have experienced and/or witnessed many of the dimensions and qualities of Dr. Honig, many of which I review with positive regard. Others I had some question or debate about. I have seen him do fine and moving things, moments I don't quite know how to describe. Of the many things that happened at The Clinic, for any negative comments or events about which you may have heard, I could easily tell you any number of instances where something of a positive nature took place.

And so, too, my experience of or with Dr. Honig. I have seen him spend hour after hour dealing with an intensely needy person, thoughtfully probe the issue at a case conference or debate, easily working out of doors with a crew of patients, rambling down the court with a group of staff and residents at the weekly sports events he helped to organize. And on and on.

Dr. Honig is a man dealing with very serious, intense, and often complex matters and, perhaps, as frequently happens with people dealing with such critical matters, may have to make decisions or take actions which others might question, something I think which has happened with regard to a number of issues or events. Some of these matters I am not sure how to evaluate, but Dr. Honig impresses me as being the kind of man who, despite some frailties as we all possess, is still willing to take on the responsibilities and pressures of such complex and intense activities as occur at The Clinic. Add to this a man dealing with his own existence and personal needs, and the efforts required for their fulfillment, and the scope of the struggle mounts. But this is something Dr. Honig has been willing to try, and I am impressed with his perseverance. *(Unsigned*

About a month later, I received a phone call from Max's father in California. He stated that Maxwell had called him, saying everything was fine and asking if he could visit. His father agreed.

His father waited one, two, three weeks before calling the Los Angeles Police, who, in turn, put out a missing person's national alarm. After several more weeks he was requested to come to a small town near Lincoln, Nebraska, to identify the remains of a man who turned out to be his son.

The body showed signs of a severe struggle; bruises covered Max's facial area, both arms, and the left ankle, and several cervical vertebra were fractured. The gold watch was gone.

After completing the story of Maxwell, I happened to find Melville's story of Bartleby, written in the 1850s. Bartleby's posturing, his repetitive replies of "I prefer not to" when asked to do any task, his isolation, haughtiness, and obstinacy, and his final self-starvation and death in debtors' prison after abandonment by everyone, reinforced my belief that taking the drastically active role with Maxwell was indeed most probably a life-saving measure.

Interestingly, Bartleby's character evokes sympathy in some, revulsion in others. Few would describe his plight as an illness. "What I saw this morning persuaded me that might give alms to his body, but his body did not pain him. It was his soul that suffered, and his soul I could not reach."

Boundaries and Borders

I will prescribe regimen for the food of my patients
according to my ability and my judgment and never
do harm to anyone. In every home where I come, I
will enter only for the good of my patients, keeping
myself for the good of my patients, keeping myself
far from all intentional ill-doing and all seduction,
and especially from the pleasures of love with
women or with men, be they free or slaves.

Hippocrates

Upon reading these stories, there are members of the lay
public and the judicial system, and even some psychiatric
practitioners, who might raise an eyebrow at the treatment
of the four patients whose case studies I have presented.
They might wonder: Did he exceed the boundaries of
clinical practice? Did the treatment extend beyond the
normal doctor-patient relationship? Was cruel and unusual
punishment used? If so, to what means? I defend no set
theory in these stories. Different therapies can achieve
positive outcomes, and sometimes there are even cures.

Perhaps theories are never meant to be truths but
only tools that, when applied, often lead to more theories
that lead to enlightenment. With each patient, I have always
turned to the words of Hippocrates as a moral guide if I
feared my daily work practices tiptoed along the margins of
questionable behavior.

In "Hard-boiled Eggs," there were times when
compassion was called for—but never when the patient felt
worthless and undeserving. When faced with a patient's life
or death, I chose to wrestle the wild bull to the ground.

151

Cruel? Perhaps. But never did I lose empathy with the patient. Rather than commiserate, I believed that too much honey at these times would have been "sputum to the eye" or, its opposite, no effect at all.

Did I have the right to envision myself as a surgeon with a cancer to excise? Had I exceeded the boundaries of custom? Does the result (in this case, a complete reversal and cure) justify the means, the unconventional insistence on eating hard-boiled eggs?

Sitting with a patient nine to twelve hours at a stretch may indeed challenge the boundaries of consultation. Is it seduction, if not of the body, then of the mind? If so, it might be considered an immoral invasion of another's space. Or can the practice be accepted as an infusion of energy and emotion that tripped the scales of life over death?

Cradling an adult in one's lap and feeding warm bottles are normally practices in the nurturing of infants, not in therapy for adults. Yet, at times, adults have benefitted from these practices.

Tickle therapy? When combined with a kiss to the cheek, this might be considered a form of humiliation by critics. But again, at times it's been successful in treating adults.

What about an electronic machine (i.e., the Relaxicizer, that ever- present weight-reducing appliance) attached to the limbs to emotionalize a patient? Though this implement is totally unlike the instruments used in giving electric shock therapy (ECT), often for intractable depression and catatonia, the Relaxicizer and other impulse-stimulation devices have been unfairly compared to ECT.

Let us remember that the methods described here were conceived for work with inpatients, all of whom had failed in the other therapies available to them, and were carefully administered under conditions where much influence over the milieu was possible (under state regulations). With outpatients, where ability to control the environment is limited, and with patients who have much greater command of their faculties, more conventional therapies were employed.

When I graduated from medical school, I was happy to practice traditional medicine. What I didn't know seemed as vast as the galaxies. And it was fun developing and serving an ever-increasing family practice. At that time, traditional psychiatry was as dead as the Great Salt Lake. Heavy hopelessness abided in treatment of the most intransigent of the mental maladies; schizophrenia, as well as mood, obsessive, compulsive, and panic-anx iety disorders that had become chronic and intractable. Being young and in therapy, my mind was ablaze as I sought new ways to understand the dark caverns of my patients' emotions.

I applied aspects of stage theater on the scaffolding that psychoanalysis provided. Freud had confessed to Reik that he knew little about schizophrenia, and Reik, my teacher, knew little more. I turned to infant development and object-relation theory for the tools with which to work. If I was to continue with these unyielding cases, I had two alternatives: I could agree with the foreboding labels of current thinking, quit, and return to family practice; or I could accept each new and complicated case experientially with no promise or prediction. I chose the latter. This meant meeting each crisis as it occurred.

As it became known that I would not refuse difficult problems, more formidable cases arrived at The Clinic. Most of these patience had lived their illness ten years or more, and they suffered from a diverse range of illnesses.

From America's breadbasket came unsocialized farm offspring who had been forced to live, alone, in the basement of a farmhouse. Catatonics were wheeled in by elderly parents. The violent, who had languished in state institutions, came by direct transfer. (Violence in a state hospital is armor for survival, but violence in a home generates terror).

Each of these patients was placed in a cottage to taste family life. Initial therapy might include instruction in using a toilet instead of urinating in a corner of a room. The language of body care—the use of soap and toothpaste— and how to eat with a fork, spoon, and napkin (instead of just fingers) were basic and far more important for the patient to learn than the language of emotion. As treatment progressed, both became important in the building of self-esteem.

I began to see that resistance to therapy lessened in patients who lived within the protection of a surrogate family. The illness became more visible as symptoms that were reactions to the stress and obligations of daily interpersonal life. With this new viewpoint, my colleagues and myself could better understand the vast unknown of each patient.

Society was changing rapidly. The counterculture movement, giving license to new values and priorities, began slowly in the mid 1960s and churned like a steam train along the tracks of America. The movement fostered a new consciousness—an alternate society that advocated broad social changes connected directly to personal crisis.

Traditional society convulsed and reacted in an explosion that even now continues to erupt. But, as always in a clash of opposites, a blending of ingredients came about.

There is many ideas that the counter-culture movement offered back in the 1970's that could be helpful to the chronic patient even today:

1. A complete attitude change toward life may be necessary for recovery.

2. Rebellion against old institutions (family, church, law, education— those tried and true institutions that had failed these people) is not effective if attempted alone. Patients may find it more workable to be with a group, a community of people with similar problems. Fusing with others lessened isolation and provided more clout against those who were not responsive, and those in opposition to understanding the struggle of someone with mental problems.

3. The counter-culture movement emphasized and encouraged self-exploration and experimentation as being essential to self-development. It emphasized human needs over technological needs, personal rights over property rights, cooperation over competition, love over violence, distribution and sharing over self-indulgence. Personal openness was respected more than secrecy; ends became more important than means. And asylum and refuge meant more than hopelessness and isolation.

4. Generally, if people could tolerate the eccentricities of the mental patient, and have patience and

understanding, isn't it possible that all society might broaden?

Real Love in Imaginary Wagon

Well, Doctor—all my loving poems
Write themselves to you,
By gum, it's what I'd do.
And never pen another
Foolish Freudian line
That bleeds across the page
In half assed metered rhyme.

If all this bother and devotion
Is not, in truth, for you-
(Since you're the expert on emotion)
Tell me Doctor—who?

The use of regressive therapies—those that resurrect hidden memories and feelings of earlier life (nurturing bottles, hugs, holding, rocking)—should always be balanced with prescriptions of "adult" personal responsibility (prescripted interaction with others in work and socialization groups).

Physicians familiar with deep areas of the mind, where the physical and psychological interfuse, respect the concept of regression. Clinicians have worked with the phenomenon of regression over centuries, and they have found it one of the most useful tools in working with the very sick.

In regression, emotions of childhood reemerge, and can be observed, mixed with adult emotion. This gives patients the opportunity to become stronger and better able to deal with the adversities of life that they must continue to face. Regression is the 'retreat lodge' of the chronically ill.

Regression played an important role in each of the stories you read in this book. It existed in each patient's psyche and is exhibited throughout the earliest stages of treatment. Today, with managed care hustling patients through a system of behavioral normality, there is little toleration for regression. Instead, it is viewed as unwieldy;

and, since it does not often adhere to prescribed time limits, it is seen as too costly. The time may be near when the phenomenon of regression will no longer be recognized by clinicians who have become blinded by the pressure for cost-effective success.

A therapist who is overly flattered by the attentions of his or her patient may become as vulnerable as a fly in a spider's web, especially if he or she falsely believes that only he or she can save the patient. The danger of disappointment for the therapist is extreme in these cases, for no one human being can be all and everything to another human being.

Patients like Cheryl, who walk the tightrope between psychosis and neurosis, may respond to many different theories of treatment (and conflicting views of limit-setting). They are like a sponge absorbing water; their extreme need for love and attention makes them highly impressionable, sometimes overly seductive and dependent, and that makes therapy difficult.

When the needs of the physician compete with the needs of the patient, treatment will break down. The patient should never be rejected or abandoned. The overly narcissistic "lovesick therapist" may experience a loss of reality testing that forces him or her to take great risks for self-gratification. Such a therapist should seek personal consultation.

I believe it is essential that a therapist continue personal psychotherapy (thus my sessions with Dr. Adler). Often, making the effort to do so will preserve the doctor-patient balance when boundaries seem to be dissolving like steam into the air.

As for family participation, it is probably best to set the ground rules at the beginning of treatment. While most patients prefer the comfort of the patient-therapist one-to-one situation, it is usually a huge mistake to exclude a biological family from the therapy. Supportive family alliances are often formed once the family understands the patient's pathology and the doctor's case management. In the past I was able to invite family members to come and live with their grandchild, child or sibling during a crisis, thereby incorporating biologic families into the therapeutic milieu. The illness may have seeded itself through three or more generations. Isolating the family creates suspicion that could destroy treatment benefits.

Blaming mother, a scapegoat technique of the 1940s and 1950s, is no longer fashionable. Still, some therapists continue to instill guilt in mothers.

Sexual abuse now commands center stage and there is open controversy. Repressed amnestic memories have been shown to be true in some cases, false in others. Much care must be taken by a therapist, for many innocent lives have been damages where memories have proven to be tainted.

Reik occupied one room in a daughter's apartment on the Upper West Side of Manhattan. His treatment couch was also his bed. He often requested that I bring my medical bag; frequently he would interrupt the sessions to ask for an examination of his heart or gouty arthritis. I felt honored by his trust in my medical abilities. At first I wondered if such interactions exceeded therapeutic boundaries. Later I learned that his humanness and informality, probably inappropriate in general medicine, actually helped me understand psychotherapy.

The mute and catatonic schizophrenic patient may require a touch of hands to repersonalize a socially withdrawn ego. A distrusting, hostile, and potentially suicidal adolescent may need to have lunch with his or her therapist (or some similar shared activity) to foster a healthy interpersonal communication across a generational gap.

Patients who believed they were God, or who exhibited feelings of godlike omnipotence, have been particularly challenging. My questions of "Why must you be so mighty? Are you really so unimportant?" were met by expressions of disdain or aggression. After considerable observation, it became apparent to me that more powerful forces would be necessary for metamorphism. If these people were to become human again, they would have to be shaken from their deadness and reintroduced to basic human values of love and nurturance.

Those who were withdrawn, who did not sleep or eat, who were so hopeless they dared not believe life could hold any beauty or love, or to whom the slightest touch became a violation causing immense pain, responded only to intense emotional arousal. Cairns demonstrated that attachment is enhanced by the amount of contact more than by the quality or intensity of the stimuli. Interestingly, he found that noxious stimuli enhance attachment.

There are critical periods in a child's development when needs are magnified, and some of these needs are even universal. For example, the bonding that takes place between mother and infant immediately after birth is critical to further emotional growth. Other critical times may vary with each child. If there is little recognition or understanding of these needs, the child will be left wanting. This may result in weakened development, a weakened, picked- on child, and an immature adult. Early recognition makes the problem easier to correct.

Many times my wife, a trained family therapist, and I have found it helpful to patients to meet with their families away from the Clinic when families were unable to visit their inpatient child, mate, or sibling. Working as a team, we have stayed with and treated whole families for short periods of time in many parts of the world.

No therapist can completely replace a parent. Parental experience (whether good or bad) in critical periods of early life is probably imprinted and is almost impossible to erase. At best, the therapist recognizes and fills emotional voids.

Rarely do I restrict phone calls from patients to my home. Hopefully, these calls will be productive, a sharing of thoughts, feelings, dreams. Gathering information between visits helps me to better know my patient.

Families who have seen many methods of treatment with minimal results, will often demand a new or alternative therapeutic experience. Some of these therapies may traverse the borders and boundaries of the rule books. There always have been those therapists who could find another way to create another chance for the patient.

The basic training I received in the osteopathic school of medicine added both a sensitive portal to my patients and a way to challenge the boundaries of orthodoxy. I had chosen the osteopathic over the more traditive and influential allopathic school of medicine. Emphasizing maintenance, enhancement, and recovery of health through the patient's own inherent resources—the physician within and the body's own medicines—the osteopathic approach allowed both freedom from the restraints of convention and a hands-on awareness of diagnosis and treatment.

Unlike the infectious diseases, the chronic degenerative diseases cannot be ascribed to a single eradicable cause. Their etiologies are complex, the products of whole constellations of factors in the ways and circumstances in which one lives and has lived. The contributing elements may be in a variety of realms—subjective as well as objective—genetic, developmental, psychologic, perceptual, sociocultural, structural, nutritional, environmental.

The degenerative diseases are the totally natural culmination of living on physiological paths that are unfavorable in various ways. The only hope for enduringly effective treatment and for prevention and lowered probability is to move patients and the not-yet-sick to more favorable life paths. By the time most mental disorders are recognized by professionals, they are, for the most part, chronic degenerative illnesses.

Osteopathic theory expounds holism—the whole person—as opposed to reductionism—mechanistic biomedical philosophy. Reductionism teaches that the best way, perhaps the only way, to understand anything, including humans, their illnesses, and the origins of their vulnerability, is to take them apart, reduce them to components, study these parts and their interactions, find out the cause of dysfunction, and find a chemical or physical agent to set the parts right. The reductionist approach dominates medical research and has been enormously productive, the source of many of our greatest medical discoveries. It is at the heart of scientific medicine and modern medical education. But will it ever be enough to understand all the complexities of the human mind? Does it consider different human environments, belief systems, and their effects on human emotions to be of equal importance? So far, these questions remain unanswered.

Conclusion

If I have freedom in my love,
And in my soul am free,
Angels alone that soar above
Enjoy such liberty.

Lovelace, "To Althea from Prison"

"Come in, the door is always open," I say to former patients. When they call or visit, they always ask about other patients, houseparents, and family assistants (aides) that they have lived with. I do not always have the information on their whereabouts, for forty years may divide into eight or nine segments of time. "Tell me the names of your housemates." I say to them. One or two names can be the key to a closetful of memories.

Many former patients have settled nearby, even if their families were from another part of the country. I would like to believe that their relationship to The Clinic, my wife, or myself was so intense, that they have arrogated us as family.

On occasion someone will make an appointment for an hour of therapy. However, most encounters are informal. A chance meeting in the supermarket or the local cinema, an invitation to a child's birthday party.

When we speak, it is as friends, as much as the generation gap allows. We talk of child rearing, careers, swimming lessons, little league, nursery school. Both my wife and I (she worked with the same patients in art therapy) are looked upon as older family members, and we use our generational influence to help with jobs, school admissions, and in other ways that we can be effective.

I probably will always remain sad when I think of Maxwell. For he has a special place in my memory. I dared to believe in him, not only as a friend, but also as a colleague. We were almost there.

The demanding around-the-clock devotion to patients housed at The Clinic began insidiously to take its toll. The long hours away, the missed family dinners, the loss of time with my own children, the cry of "You are never home" were bullets to the chest.

The all-night calls, the tension of risk taking that often took patients and myself to the very edge, the immense power of life and death, began to wear. I never stopped pouring all my emotion into the work. It was I who now was feeling the stress. Sleepless nights, esophagitis, tonsillitis, colitis, and increased prostate infections. The prostate and the tonsils had always been my stress points.

I asked the Board of Directors to find another medical director. I began to make plans for retirement and, within a year, left The Clinic.

I continue to treat patients; now in an office that is in our home. In semiretirement, my day is full—writing, gardening, restoring old cars. I attend case conferences at The Clinic. Here, I've been asked to interview patients before a polyglot of psychiatrists, social workers, nurses, and house therapists. My many years' experience working with patients, treating with or without medication, is respected and sought after.

One cottage still has houseparents. The marketing department brings all prospective patients and their families to this cottage. It is the show place. Most parents feel safer leaving their sick member with a real family in a true home rather than in the dormitory (eight-hour-shift work cottages).

There are other changes. With my leaving and the ushering in of managed care, The Clinic has a new name. Nursing stations sit in each cottage. One cottage has been enlarged and made into an admission unit.

No longer are restraints a therapeutic venue. No longer are violent patients bundled in restraints and included in the family constellation of group sessions, living room life, eating with the family. Each cottage now has a time-out room to contain the violent.

When I go to The Clinic today, for medical staff meetings or to tend the large vegetable and flower garden, I remember where the greenhouse stood; it is now a baseball field. I see the new gymnasium that sits where the sweet corn once grew. Patients, whose stays are measured one day at a time, get much more use from a baseball field or basketball court than from a garden where they can learn to grow their own food. It takes a season for plants to grow.

As I scan the borders of what was once two farms and see the large black locust trees, I can still remember the patients and staff planting the little seedlings. The swamp maple with its starburst of spreading limbs has grown larger and stronger. With arms extended it beckons all to the safety of its bosom. It sits at the center of circling cottages, and with its benches full of lounging patients and staff, it looks like the central square of a small European village, the way it was originally designed.

I remain with many concerns about my profession:

Like all of medicine, psychiatry is in the throes of a revolution. This time it is not a revolution of the spirit, but of management efficiency and cost containment. All medical practice has become subjugated to a business strategy in the service of a competitive marketplace—commonly labeled "managed care." Like it or not, for the near term, the number of Americans enrolled in managed competition programs will probably continue to increase. Have psychiatry and its allied mental health fields fared well in this revolution? Perhaps in some ways. The health maintenance organizations have been able to reduce their mental health budgets from a national norm of ten percent to as little as two percent. But this has resulted in devastating consequences for the patients with serious mental disorders.

With managed care, psychiatrists are limited to assessment and prescription of antipsychotic medications, yet held responsible for the supervision of psychotherapy administered by nonmedical personnel.

In an effort to monitor practice and unify delivery, one of the demands of standardization, the American Psychiatric Association has developed guidelines of psychiatric practice. Perhaps they will elevate care in a general sense, but they no doubt will also dampen innovation.

For example: few patients will be offered treatment that doesn't include medication. In fact, any doctor who treats without medication could be open to a lawsuit. However, as the stories written here show, there will always be patients who want to be treated without medication. Should they have that right if they have the judgment to make that decision?

Hospitals have changed. The shortened stays, the disappearance of nonverbal and creative therapies (music, art, dance, and psychodrama) that once were considered important in the search for self-identity either are not considered important, or are too costly. Patients do not stay long enough, so there is little time for exploration or reparenting.

Genes, and newer and better medications, are all important, but they are not the magic bullet. The nature-nurture bifurcation (choose: biology or environment) is an illusion. Scholars now feel that ''nurture'' is dependent on biology and genetic makeup, and every aspect of our biology from brain development to food preference has been shaped by an environment.

Of practical concern is the steadily declining number of medical graduates interested in working with the severely mentally ill. Everybody seems disgusted with the system.

The psychotherapy of the severely mentally ill is an art form traditionally practiced by a small number of therapists. It is taught by apprenticeship, and not learned from books. Its teachers are aging and the clinics where it was practiced are vanishing. Soon there will be no masters left. No masters, no students to learn. No practitioners of the art, no patients and families—the consumers will soon forget that intensive psychologic treatment ever existed as an option.

But there are some hopeful signs. Although research has lagged far behind genetics and biology, encouraging studies are demonstrating the effectiveness of the psychotherapies. For instance, psychotherapy over a three-year period decreased relapses and the revolving-door rehospitalization frequently common with drug therapy alone. Also, long-term relationship therapy is showing to be more effective than brief therapy. Surprisingly, long-term inpatient care may be more cost effective than short, frequent, managed hospitalizations. With more inpatient care, quality of life and patient satisfaction have been shown to increase.

What's the answer?

A society has always been measured by how it treats its poor, its jailed, and its mentally ill.

I call for the establishment of a system, organized by each state, that would set aside one house in each community in which houseparents would reside with up to four seriously ill mental patients from the community.

Early intervention, biologic family involvement (including three generations and extended family), and professional supervision would create a dynamic open milieu that could incorporate all advances in psychiatry (including medications and new genetic findings). Openness would eliminate shame, blame, and stigma, and it would feed back information that would enable the community itself to mature.

Change is exciting. Interpolating old ideas, when proven workable, into a new system is of immense value, and fun. For now, I continue to enjoy working with the chronic patient in what ways are available, still appreciating the freedom to be creative. Hopefully, readers of this book will be inspired to breathe new life into the long tradition of psychotherapy with the severely mentally ill.

Notes

Author's Preface

1. Simmons, A. 10th Annual R. Carter Symposium on Mental Health Policy, *Psychiatric Times,* 2/95 p.26. About 5 million Americans (2.8 percent of the adult population, 13 percent of children) experience severe mental disorders during a one-year period. Seventy percent of the children never receive needed treatment. The suicide rate among 10- to 19-year-olds increased 30 percent between 1980 and 1989. Costs for treating these disorders can be astronomical. The nation pays an estimated $20 billion a year (with an additional $7 billion a year for nursing home charges). These figures represent four percent of total U.S. direct health care costs. When the social expenses are included, severe mental disorders exact an annual financial toll of $74 billion. This total accounts for the dollar costs of shortened lives and lost productivity, as well as the amounts incurred in the criminal justice and social service systems.

2. Health Care Reform for Americans with Severe Mental Illnesses: Report of the National Advisory Mental Health Council, *Am. Journal of Psychiatry* 150:10 Oct. 93. Private health insurance coverage for mental disorders is often limited to 10-30 inpatient days per year, compared with 120 days or unlimited days for physical illnesses. Similarly, the Medicare program required 50 percent co-payment for outpatient care of mental disorders compared with 20 percent co-payment for other medical outpatient treatment. Recently, however, there has been an approach toward parity.

Chapter I

1. Gull, W.W. (1868) Anorexia Nervosa in

165

Evolution of Psychosomatic Concepts, *Anorexia Nervosa: A Paradigm*, ed. M. Kaufman and M. Heiman Inter. Un. Press, 1964.

2. Bruch, H., *The Golden Cage, The Enigma of Anorexia Nervosa,* Harvard U. Press, Cambridge, MA 1978.

3. Foss, M., *The Founding of the Jesuits,* 1540. Weybright and Talley NY, 1969.

4. Sacks, 0., *Man who Mistook his Wife for a Hat,* preface, p. viii, Harper & Row NY, 1970.

5. Davis, A., *Let's Have Healthy Children,* Harcourt, Brace Jovanovich Inc., NY, 1972.

6. Nurturing bottles of warm sweet milk reactivate lost sensations around mouth, chest, and upper abdomen. A. Honig, Psychotherapy with Command Hallucinations, *JGPPS*, Spring, 1991, p.13.

7. Psychological therapies are still the treatment of choice. These include psychotherapy (Bruch), psychoanalysis (Mintz, Mushatt, Spurs, Sperling, Thom Wilson), family systems therapies (Menuchin, Palazolli), and object relations therapy (Bettleheim, Cohler). Wilson states that without resolution of the underlying personality disorder which can only happen with psychoanalysis, there is always danger of relapse. All other improvements with any other kind of treatment are labeled transference cures—from Wilson's *Fear of Being Fat.* I fully understand that the treatment that I am to embark upon is highly unconventional and therefore risky. I am prepared to abandon all of it if the patient's condition worsens.

8. Psychoanalytic interpretations are not favored by Bruch or Palazzoli. Sperling says that the establishment and maintenance of a workable transference with these patients is no easy task, and can only be established by frustrating the patient's need to turn the analyst into mother *(Fear of Being Fat).* Insight (the registration in the unconscious of past patterns and their consequences), both intellectual and emotional, has been a goal of psychoanalytic therapies (Hammer E., *Use of Interpretation in Treatment,* Grune and Stratton, NY, 1968) that has many detractors. Criticisms have emerged such as "the patient spent 20 years on the couch, knows everything about him/herself, but feels nor functions no better for all the time spent in

treatment".

9. M. Sperling and others have highlighted the onset of pathology with the birth of a sibling, most often a brother. Ann's attachment to mother had always been weak (ambivalent); she experienced the new birth as a further rejection (*Fear of Being Fat*, p. 54).

10. Mintz,L, *Fear of Being Fat*.

11. Schonbar, R., *Interpretation and Insight in Psychotherapy from Use of Interpretation in Treatment;* Hammer (ed). Grune & Stratton, 1968.

12. Hobbs, N., Sources of Gain in Psychotherapy. *Amer. Psycho.*, 1962, 17, 741-747.

13. *Journal of Group Psychotherapy, Psychodrama, and Sociometry,* Heldref Publications, Washington, DC

14. Honig, A., Psychotherapy with Command Hallucinations in Chronic Schizophrenia; The Use of Action Techniques within a Surrogate Family Setting, *Jr. of Group Psychotherapy, Psychodrama & Sociometry*.

Chapter II

1. Plath, S., Lesbos (1962) p. 255-257. *The Art of Sylvia Plath,* ed. by C. Newman, Indiana U. Press, Bloomington, 1970.

2. Plath, S., (1962), p. 255-257. *The Art of Sylvia Plath,* ed. by C. Newman, Indiana U. Press, Bloomington, 1970.

3. Plath, S., Two Views of a Cadaver Room, *The Times Literary Supplement* #3010 (Nov. 6, 1959), 29.

4. *The Confessions of St. Augustine,* trans. by E. Pusey, Washington Press, 1960.

5. Sexton, A., *Live or Die,* pp. 58-59. Houghton & Miflin, Boston, 1966.

6. Sexton, A., *Sylvia's Death for Sylvia Plath*, 2/17. 1963, p. 38, Live or Die.

7. Fromm-Reichmann, *Psychotherapy with Schizophrenics,* International Universities Press, NY, 1952.

8. Rosen, J., *Direct Analysis,* Grune & Stratton, NY, 1953.

9. Hillman, J., *Suicide and the Soul,* Harper & Row,

NY, 1964.

10. Honig, A., Negative Transference in *Psychosis,Psychoanalysis, and Psychoanalytical Review* 47(4); 105-114.

11. Bergman, I., *Face to Face - a Film*. Pantheon Books (Random House), NY, 1976.

12. Ullman, L., *Changing,* Bantam Books, NY. pp. 135-137.

13. Stengel, E., Cook, N. and Kreeger, I., *Attempted Suicide,* London, 1958. 14. During the years of Cheryl Henderson's querre a' mort, the working diagnosis had been major suicidal depression, with considerable residual symptomatic and social impairment. In due course, that label no longer fit. Perhaps we were born twenty years too soon, before borderlines and that exotic pill of pills, Prozac, was fashionable. Prozac was one of the first synthesized compounds that selectively inhibit the reuptake of the neurotransmitter serotonin. It was introduced before the new age of "the bounties of science when a drug's effect is global—extending social popularity, business acumen, self - image, energy, flexibility, and sexual appeal" (Kramer P., *Listening to Prozac,* Viking Press, NY, 1994), when it causes not just a healing affect but a transformation, with little side effects. Borderline personality disorder became respectable as a diagnostic entity in the late 1970s. All borderlines show ego weakness, lack of anxiety tolerance, lack of impulse control, splitting (creating people into goodies and baddies), primitive idealization, and regression of the personality. Yet individual borderlines are different. Some are agoraphobic, others psychopathic; some are loners, others intolerant of aloneness. Some show little affect, others crave sensation and seek to escape chronic boredom. Some are naive and trusting, others paranoid. Many have a history of child abuse or self mutilation. Because of the grab bag of symptoms, the diagnosis is blurred. If parents killed themselves, forty percent of the offspring end their own lives. Prognosis runs the gamut from good to poor. Outcome is difficult to predict. The struggle between separation from the past and trying to make a new life after hospitalization is critical, and I have worked with patients who got a glimpse of reality and retreated. Good treatment results have been reported with

behavior modification, medication, and expressive psychotherapies, both alone and in combination (Stone, MH. Update on Borderline Disorders, Disorders Diagnostic, and Treatment Issues, a Tape, c. 1987, Smith, Kline Beckman). Most authorities agree that therapy with borderlines is both time consuming and demanding. They may absorb, imitate, or clone others' personalities, creating a difficult management problem. Boundary distinction between therapist and patient becomes fuzzy. I venture to say that Cheryl fit the nomenclature of a borderline. That is, after she gave up her need to die.

Chapter III

1. The Sieur Louis de Compte, *Personal Recollections of Joan of Arc,* 1492. Translated by Jean Francois Alden Nelson, Doubleday Inc., Garden City, NY.
2. Kaplan, H., & Sadock, B., *Handbook of Clinical Psychiatry,* pp. 265-269, Williams and Wilkins, Baltimore, 1990 Electric Convulsive Therapy: Usually reserved for patients who have failed other treatments or who are so acutely dangerous or suicidal that a course of pharmacotherapy might be too slow. E.C.T. is most effective in depression, controversial in schizophrenia, and treatment of choice in pregnancy where psychotropic drugs might be dangerous to mother and baby. E.C.T. can cause cardiac arrhythmia (occasionally death), and prolonged seizures resulting in memory impairment. Memory loss is usually temporary, but can be permanent where treatments are extensive (75 or more). Procedure: Electrodes are placed bilaterally over the temple areas of the skull. A surge of current is introduced into the brain. This induces a seizure of 35-80 seconds. When the patient awakes, there is amnesia regarding the event. Joan's parents and her physicians saw diminishing returns as the treatments continued. They feared permanent damage if the treatments continued past the 40 or so mark thatm she received, and so sought an alternative. Thus the referral to the clinic.
3. Hall, L.L., *NAMI Advocate* Vol. 17 #3, Arlington, VA.
4. Szas, T.S., *The Myth of Mental Illness,* Hoeber

Harper, NY, 1964.

5. One half of obsessives are obsessed with dirt, contamination, germs, and bugs. These people are identified by chafed, dry, reddened hands—victims of uncontrollable hand washing or a need to continually check things like locked doors or gas stoves (Rachman, S.J. and Hogdson, R.J., *Obsessions and Compulsions,* Prentice - Hall, Englewood Cliff, NJ, 1980). About one-fourth have repetitive, intrusive thoughts that cover over horrifying impulses. Excessive doubt causes compulsive "trying to make things right" thoughts. Trying to fight these excesses makes it difficult to concentrate and exhaustion results. Diagnosis becomes difficult when neurotic doubts about sinfulness become delusions of persecutions, and intrusive thoughts emerge into auditory hallucinations. When patients embrace rather than resist these inner voices, and the intrusive thoughts acquire the qualities of delusions (the absolute obedience to perform rituals is not dissimilar to the subjugation of command hallucinations), a diagnosis of Obsessive Compulsive Disorder with psychotic features is made (Insel, T. and Akiskal, H.,, Obsessive Compulsive Disorder with Psychotic Features: A Phenomenologic Analysis *Am. Journal Psychiatry*, 143:12 Cec. 1986).

6. NIMH researcher, Personal communication, 1991.

7. Compte, *Personal Recollections of Joan of Arc,* Ch. 17.

8. Williams, D., et al, *Infants in Multi-risk Families, A Case of Double Vulnerability for Mother and Child;* Louise and Robbie, ed. Greenspan S., Int. U. Press, Madison, CN, 1987.

9. *Joan of Arc,* p. 11

10. The Sieur Louis de Compte, *Personal Recollections of Joan of Arc,* ch. 22, 1493., N. Doubleday, Garden City, NY.

11. Gilles de La Tourette's Syndrome - Motor coordination with Echolalia and Coprolalia (Foul language or cursing), *Stedman's Medical Dictionary,* 25th Ed., Williams and Wilkins, Baltimore, 1990.

12. *Personal Recollections of Joan of Arc,* Compte, xx

13. Compte.

14. Compte, pg. 50

Chapter IV

1. How To Save the Homeless - and Ourselves. Pete Hamill, *New York Magazine,* Sept. 20, 1993, pp. 35-39.

2. Bettleheim B., *The Informed Heart,* Avon Books.

3. Hippocrates

4. Isakower O., Contributions to the Psychopathology of Falling Asleep, *Int. Jr. of Psychoanalysis* 13:331-345, 1938.

5. Pavlov I., *Essays in Psychology and Psychiatry,* Citadel Press, NY 1962.

6. Honig, A. Psychotherapy with Command Hallucinations in Chronic Schizophrenia: The Use of Action Techniques Within a Surrogate Family Setting, *Jr. of Group Psychotherapy, Psychodrama & Sociometry,* Spring, 1991.

7. Khan, M., The Concept of Cumulative Trauma, *The Psychoanalytic Study of the Child* 18:286-306, 1963.

8. Freud, A., Assessment of Childhood Disturbances, *Psychoanalytic Study of the Child,* 17:149-158, 1962.

9. Swedenborg, E., *Spiritual Diary,* James Speirs, 1883, London.

10. James, W., *The Varieties of Religious Experience,* Mentor Books, NY, 1958.

11. Sargant, W., *Battle for the Mind,* Harper & Row, NY, 1959.

12. Mandala, the Hindu word for magic circle, was to the Navaho Indian the way to bring the sick back to harmony with themselves and with the cosmos, thereby restoring health. With mandala structured sand paintings, they attempted to restore an inner balance. In Eastern civilizations, similar pictures are used to consolidate one's inner being, or to enable one to plunge into deep meditation. A contemplation of a mandala is meant to bring inner peace and a rediscovery of meaning to life.

13. Cairns, R., Attachment Behavior in Mammals, *The Psychological Review,* 1966, vol. 73 #5, pp. 409-426.

14. Leonard, E., Early Cures at Friends Hospital, *Psychiatric News,* Jan. 21,1994, p. 10.

15. Melville, H.S, *Selected Writings,* Bartleby, pp. 3-47, quote from p. 25. The Modern Library, Random House, NY, 1952.

Boundaries and Borders

1. Electroconvulsive therapy- a treatment of mental disorders where convulsions are produced by the passage of an electric current through the brain. *Stedman's Medical Dictionary* 25th ed., Williams and Wilkins, Baltimore 1990.

2. Reik, T. *Personal Communication* 1959.

3. Brazelton, B., *Infants and Mothers,* Delta/Seymour Lawrence, NY, 1983; Stern, D., *The Interpersonal World of the Infant.* Basic Books NY, 1985; Greenspan S., *Infants in Multi-risk Families,* Int. Univ. Press, Conn. 1987; Bowlby J., *Child Care and the Growth of Love,* Penguin Books, Baltimore, 1953.

4. Klein, M. and Riviere,J., Love, Hate, and Reparation, WW Norton, NY, 1964.

5. Look Mag., April, 1966.

6. Freud, S. Thoughts for the Time on War and Death. *Collected Works,* London, Hogarth 1957, vol.14 p 273-274.

7-9. Hig A. *The Awakening Nightmare.* p.70. American Faculty Press. Rockaway NJ 1972.

10. Gersten, S. in *Mcnama E's Breakdown,* p.231 Pocket Books, NY,1994

11.Wylie, P., *Generation of Vipers,* Farrat and Rinehart, NY 1942.

12. Pearlman, T., Depersonalizing Psychotherapy, *Clinical Psychiatry News,* Feb., 1995.

13. Freud, S., Fragment of an Analysis of a case of Hysteria - Dora., . 1905, CP.III, 13, Standard Ed., 7,3.

14. Cairns, R. Attachment Behavior in Mammals, *The Psychological Review,* 1966, vol. 7 #5 pp. 409-426.

15. Cairns, R. Attachment Behavior in Mammals, *The Psychological Review,* 1966, vol. 7 #5 pp. 409-426.

16. Korr, I., Osteopathic Medicine: The Professional Role in Society, JAOA, vol. 90, #9 Sept., 1990 pp.824-37.

17. Korr, I., Osteopathic Research: The Needed Paradigm Shift, JAOA, vol. 91, #2 Feb. 1991, pp. 156-61.,

Chicago.

18. Korr, I., Medical Education, The Resistance to Change, JAW, vol. 88, #8, Aug., 1988, Chicago

Conclusion

1. Panzetta A., *The Role of the Psychiatrist: Managed Care View in Allies and Adversaries: The Impact of Managed Care on Mental Health Services*, ed. by Schreter R.K., Sharfstein S.S., Schreter, C.A., Washington, D.C., Amer. Psych.Press. in press.

2. Freeman, M., High Quality Behavioral Health Benefit Programs are possible, but problems must be fixed first. *Managed Healthcare News,* Apr. 1993, p. 43.

3.Honig, A., *The Awakening Nightmare,* p. 70, American Faculty Press, Rockaway, NY 1972.

4.Freud, S., Thoughts for the Time on War and Death. *Collected Works,* London, Hogarth, 1957 vol. 14, pp. 273-274.

5.Meltzer, H., Young Investigators Present Schizophrenia Research by Brown, A. *Psychiatric Times,* Jan. 1995 p.12.

6.Honig A. Psychotherapy with Command Hallucinations in Chronic Schizoprenia. The Use of Action Techniques within a Surrogate Family Setting, *Jr. Group Psychotherapy, Psychodrama, and Sociometry.* Spring, 1991.

7.Moran, M. Genome Project Promises to Transform Medicine. *Psychiatric News,* March 3, 1995.

8.*Newsweek*, March 27, 1995. It's Time to Rethink Nature and Nurture, pp. 52-53.

9.Marder, S., Highlights of the 46th Institute on Hospital and Community Psychiatry, *Psychiatric Services,* Jan,, 1995, vol. #1, p.23.

10. Psychiatric residents report diminished experience in supervised psychotherapy. They are told by faculty that "there is no point in learning skills for which they will not get reimbursed." Scully. J., A Developing Crisis in Training, *Psychiatric News,* July 21, 1995, p.3.

11. Hogarty G., et al. *Three Year Trials of Personal Therapy Among Schizophrenic Patients Living With or*

Independent of Family, 1: Description of Study and Adjustment of Patients.